CONTENTS

S. Hrg. 103–1036

OVERSIGHT OF U.S.-JAPAN AUTO PARTS FRAMEWORK NEGOTIATIONS: WHAT'S NEEDED TO GET RESULTS

HEARING

BEFORE THE

SUBCOMMITTEE ON OVERSIGHT OF GOVERNMENT MANAGEMENT

OF THE

COMMITTEE ON GOVERNMENTAL AFFAIRS UNITED STATES SENATE

ONE HUNDRED THIRD CONGRESS

SECOND SESSION

FEBRUARY 3, 1994

Printed for the use of the Committee on Governmental Affairs

U.S. GOVERNMENT PRINTING OFFICE

76–349 CC WASHINGTON : 1995

For sale by the U.S. Government Printing Office
Superintendent of Documents, Congressional Sales Office, Washington, DC 20402
ISBN 0-16-047227-X

COMMITTEE ON GOVERNMENTAL AFFAIRS

JOHN GLENN, Ohio, *Chairman*

SAM NUNN, Georgia	WILLIAM V. ROTH, Jr., Delaware
CARL LEVIN, Michigan	TED STEVENS, Alaska
JIM SASSER, Tennessee	WILLIAM S. COHEN, Maine
DAVID PRYOR, Arkansas	THAD COCHRAN, Mississippi
JOSEPH I. LIEBERMAN, Connecticut	JOHN McCAIN, Arizona
DANIEL K. AKAKA, Hawaii	ROBERT F. BENNETT, Utah
BYRON L. DORGAN, North Dakota	

Leonard Weiss, *Staff Director*
Franklin G. Polk, *Minority Staff Director and Chief Counsel*
Michal Sue Prosser, *Chief Clerk*

SUBCOMMITTEE ON OVERSIGHT OF GOVERNMENT MANAGEMENT

CARL LEVIN, Michigan, *Chairman*

DAVID PRYOR, Arkansas	WILLIAM S. COHEN, Maine
JOSEPH I. LIEBERMAN, Connecticut	TED STEVENS, Alaska
DANIEL K. AKAKA, Hawaii	THAD COCHRAN, Mississippi
SAM NUNN, Georgia	JOHN McCAIN, Arizona
BYRON L. DORGAN, North Dakota	ROBERT F. BENNETT, Utah

Linda J. Gustitus, *Staff Director and Chief Counsel*
Paul Brubaker, *Minority Staff Director*
Frankie de Vergie, *Chief Clerk*

OVERSIGHT OF U.S.-JAPAN AUTO PARTS FRAMEWORK NEGOTIATIONS: WHAT'S NEEDED TO GET RESULTS

THURSDAY, FEBRUARY 3, 1994

U.S. SENATE,
SUBCOMMITTEE ON OVERSIGHT OF GOVERNMENT MANAGEMENT, COMMITTEE ON GOVERNMENTAL AFFAIRS,
Washington, DC.

The Subcommittee met, pursuant to notice, at 9:38 a.m., in room SD–562, Dirksen Senate Office Building, Hon. Carl Levin, Chairman of the Subcommittee, presiding.

Present: Senator Levin.

Staff Present: Linda J. Gustitus, Staff Director and Chief Counsel; Frankie de Vergie, Chief Clerk; and Alison Pascale, Legislative Assistant to Senator Levin.

OPENING STATEMENT OF SENATOR LEVIN

Senator LEVIN. The Subcommittee will come to order. Good morning, everybody.

Our hearing today is going to review the ongoing auto parts negotiations currently being conducted under the so-called U.S.-Japan Framework for a New Economic Partnership. That agreement was signed in Tokyo in July of 1993.

The auto parts framework negotiations, as they are called, have a self-imposed February 11th deadline, at which time President Clinton and Prime Minister Hosokawa will meet to measure progress that has been made towards meeting the agreed-to objective of increasing sales of U.S.-made auto parts and autos in Japanese markets.

Last July, both countries agreed that the negotiations will have the objective of "achieving significantly expanded sales opportunities to result in a significant expansion of purchases of foreign parts by Japanese firms in Japan and through their transplants, as well as removing problems which affect market access, and encouraging imports of foreign autos and auto parts in Japan." The Tokyo agreement also called for "significant reductions" in Japan's trade surplus and promised to assess progress "based upon sets of objective criteria."

Today we are going to hear from a chief U.S. auto and auto parts negotiator, Jeffrey Garten, of the Department of Commerce. He is Under Secretary for International Trade, and he will report to us on the status of the negotiations.

The U.S. auto parts sector is a diverse, $100 billion industry with 4,000 firms directly employing over 700,000 people. It accounts for about 11 percent of all U.S. corporate R&D and employs approximately 6 percent of all scientists and engineers in the country. It is an industry that is competitive internationally, and in 1992, excluding Japan, the United States had a $3.8 billion auto parts trade surplus with the rest of the world.

But the picture has been starkly different with respect to our auto parts trade with Japan, and let us look at the data. While high-level, market-opening talks, including the MOSS talks, have been taking place from the early 1980s to the present, the U.S. auto parts deficit with Japan has grown from roughly $1 billion in 1981 to $11 billion today.

So while the conversations have been taking place for 12 years or so, the deficit has gotten worse. Interestingly enough, as we will see later on, as the increase in so-called purchases of American parts by Japanese companies has increased, in fact, the trade deficit has gotten worse. We are going to see why that is true a little later on.

Over 50 percent of our U.S.-Japan trade deficit since 1986 is attributable to autos and auto parts—that figure is 60 percent for the 1993 deficit—and a consistent 20 percent of the total bilateral deficit is in auto parts alone. And that deficit has been growing, despite dramatic changes in the yen-dollar ratios in recent years, which gives American auto parts a significant, even a greater price advantage over Japanese auto parts.

Another fact: only 2 percent of Japan's auto parts market is comprised of foreign auto parts. Now that is compared with over 30 percent in the U.S. In other words, our auto parts market is 30 percent imported, France's is 49 percent, Germany's is 25 percent, England's is 60 percent, and Japan's is 2 percent.

Every President since President Nixon claimed Japan was about to open its markets, but those markets are still not open. In 1971 President Nixon said, "Japan has accelerated its program of liberalizing its restrictions on imports." At that time, the U.S. deficit with Japan was only $1.3 billion a year total. Today, our bilateral trade deficit with Japan is about $58 billion, and auto parts makes up a significant part of that.

Because the United States has been involved in market-opening automotive negotiations with Japan since the 1980s, with only a growing trade deficit to show for its efforts, I believe there are two critical steps that the administration must take before the February 11th summit, if it hopes to achieve real results.

First, Japan must be informed of the actions that we will take, if there is no meaningful agreement on opening their markets. Let us be clear, we are talking about opening their markets, and we have been talking about that for over 20 years. That is the issue, how to force open the Japanese auto parts market. That is what all the talking has been about for 25 years. We have not done anything significant about it yet. Our deficit has gone up during that time. But that is what the goal is, to open up their market.

Now, some are going to say our goal is to protect our markets. It is not. It is to allow our auto parts manufacturers to compete in Japan and with Japanese automobiles wherever they are built.

Here are the two things we have got to do if we are going to break open those markets. We have got to let them know what actions we are going to take, if there is no meaningful agreement on opening their markets.

Now, my preference long has been that continuing restrictions on our products will lead to equivalent restrictions on their products. Europe has taken that kind of action. They finally gave up trying to change Japanese restrictions on their products, and they just simply imposed a limit on the growth of Japanese autos not to exceed 16 percent of the European market by 1999.

I think that is the fastest and surest way to end restrictions on our products. Nobody has called the European decision to reciprocate protectionism. That seems to be accepted everywhere. The Europeans gave up on trying to open up the Japanese market to their products, and they said, OK, we are putting an equivalent restriction on your products; it is 16 percent.

In any event, whether or not we are going to notify them in advance of the actions we are going to take if they refuse to open their markets to our products and end their keiretsu system, we must decide in advance what action we will take if negotiations fail. And, equally important, we must notify Japan of that action in advance. Otherwise, negotiations will fail.

Second, the talks must produce specific commitments by Japanese manufacturers to increase purchases of previously excluded U.S. products and, in addition to those commitments and goals being set, we need specific, valid measures. We do not have specific measurements to which they are committed, and we will see more of that later on this morning.

If we cannot achieve real commitments to open their markets with specific numbers, specific criteria, specific goals, specific measurements by February 11th, I believe we should walk away from the table and call those negotiations a failure.

The worst thing we can do is just simply have another fuzzed-over agreement and to try to pass that as progress, pretend it is progress and leave those negotiations. That is the worst thing we can do. If we cannot achieve anything significant and real, we should say so.

Now, there is precedent for Japan to agree to specific goals for increasing purchases of U.S. auto parts. In January of 1992, Prime Minister Miyazawa and President Bush announced the Global Partnership Plan of Action, the so-called "action plan." It included Japanese car companies' voluntary purchase plans for U.S. auto parts, which was to be $19 billion. We are going to hear a lot about that $19 billion figure a little bit later this morning. That action plan that was agreed to between the Japanese Prime Minister and our President also included commitments to increase the percentage of parts made and assembled in the U.S. in the total Japanese transplant purchase of parts from about 50 percent to about 70 percent by 1994.

These 1994 goals are a starting point, and the Japanese manufacturers should be held to them. But even if the 1994 voluntary plans are met by the Japanese vehicle manufacturers, which is dubious, they are far less significant than they appear to be. That is because they lump together and treat as the same, purchases of components made up mainly of U.S. parts and purchases of components made up mainly of Japanese parts. It is all lumped together.

You can have a component sold by a Japanese-affiliated parts supplier, here, in the United States which has nothing more on it than a label or a tightening of single screw in the United States. All the rest could come from Japan, and that is called an American auto part, if it is sold in the United States to a transplant by a Japanese-affiliated auto parts company in the United States. It is all lumped together. That is called an American auto part, because it is bought here.

By no reasonable measure is that an American auto part. The vast majority of components bought here by transplants, in fact, have as their source parts that come from Japan that are simply assembled here. And if the vast majority of the labor and the value of that component are in fact Japanese-sourced, not American-sourced, to call that an American auto part is a farce, but that is the way it is counted.

We cannot get the real numbers as to what the American sourcing is and what the Japanese sourcing is of components that are sold in the United States by the Japanese affiliated parts companies to the transplants. We have not been able to get those numbers yet. Some of our witnesses are going to give us their assessment of those numbers later on this morning. But we need those numbers.

As of now, as I indicated, all sales to Japanese auto assembly plants by U.S.-based Japanese suppliers are counted as sales of U.S. auto parts to the Japanese. That is the reason why you can hear a transplant argue in a press release that 80 percent of a vehicle built in the U.S. is U.S. parts. The only reason they are able to make that claim, is because a significant portion of those cars contain components bought here, but a majority of those same components typically come from Japan. That is the source of the components.

We are going to try to make that point here this morning. It is a very critical point. If we make no other point here this morning, I want to make that one.

Our negotiators with the Japanese—and, again, we will hear from Jeff Garten on this—have been proposing that market-opening goals of the Japanese car makers be met by auto parts with high U.S. content, and they are proposing that we have specific measurements and that we know what the source of the components are.

If you have got a muffler that has got a label on it with a Japanese-affiliated company's name, and all that has been added in the United States is the label—just to give you an extreme example, not a real example, but one that makes the point—if all that is added is just the label and it is bought here, how in the name of common sense can we call that an American part, if most of it comes from Japan and merely the label or the last screw is tightened here? How, under any common sense definition, could that be called an American auto part, simply because it is transferred from one company to the assembly company here in the United States?

Recently, the Japanese parent companies of Japanese-affiliated auto parts suppliers in the United States have orchestrated a grass

roots effort to lobby the Administration against insisting on specific numbers, specific data and specific goals. If the Administration and the Congress cave into that lobby, the Japanese auto industry, which has restricted our auto parts and autos for decades and cost us millions of jobs, will have added a con job to the list of unfair trade practices.

Now, after 20 years of failed U.S. trade policy towards Japan, the framework negotiations provide yet another chance to provide real access to Japan's markets and to eliminate the soaring bilateral auto parts trade deficit. If we fail to live up to our rhetoric again, as we have for 25 years, Japan will have no reason to take us seriously, and its auto makers will continue to exclude U.S. auto parts suppliers at the expense of American workers and at the expense of America's manufacturing base and the health of our economy.

So I hope that, as February 11th draws near, the Administration will decide to accept nothing less than specific goals for increased Japanese purchases of U.S. made parts with high U.S. content. And if we are going to have any chance of these negotiations succeeding, the Japanese must be clearly informed what actions we will take, whatever they are going to be, whatever the Administration decides it is going to take and do. We must notify the Japanese of those actions, or else those negotiations will fail.

Now this hearing was scheduled for today as an open day on the agenda of the Governmental Affairs Committee. Yesterday, it was supposed to hear from Budget Director Leon Panetta, and he could not make it, and so the full Governmental Affairs Committee rescheduled Mr. Panetta for this morning, at the same time as this hearing, and we were unable to change this hearing. So we have a conflict, which means that a number of my colleagues who wanted to be here cannot be here, and we will, therefore, leave the record open for their questions.

Our first witness is Jeff Garten. I have already introduced him. We very much appreciate his work, his efforts, and we appreciate his being with us, here, this morning, to help us understand this issue and what our negotiating position is.

Mr. Garten?

TESTIMONY OF JEFFREY E. GARTEN,[1] UNDER SECRETARY FOR INTERNATIONAL TRADE ADMINISTRATION, U.S. DEPARTMENT OF COMMERCE

Mr. GARTEN. Thank you, Mr. Chairman.

I would like to submit a written statement for the record and just say a few words by way of introduction, and then try to answer your question.

Senator LEVIN. That would be great. Thank you.

Mr. GARTEN. This is my first official appearance in Congress since I was confirmed in November, and it is a privilege to be in front of this particular committee, and perhaps it is appropriate that the subject is Japan and automotive trade, since I have spent, I would say, two-thirds of my time since being confirmed on this issue.

[1] The prepared statement of Mr. Garten appears on page 33.

I would like to acknowledge the work of yourself and your staff and the Committee on this issue over a long period of time. I fully recognize the amount of knowledge that you all have, and I think I recognize the degree of frustration that comes with having watched the United States negotiate with Japan on these issues for such a long period of time, without satisfactory results.

I would also like to express our support for your efforts to renew the authorization of the Auto Parts Advisory Committee. This committee has been extremely useful to me and to my staff and to the administration in providing the critical private sector advice on what are some very complicated issues.

I will not go into the background of this issue, because you have summarized it very well, and I think that this committee, above all others, knows the facts, understands what we have tried to do in the past and how the trade deficit has not responded.

As you said, there has been an enormous number of efforts to deal with automotive trade from the MOSS talks, which began in 1986, to the numerous studies of the problem, to the numerous conferences which have been held, to the price surveys which show that the same parts in Japan cost multiples of what they do in the U.S., to the voluntary purchase plans.

What I would like to do just in a few minutes really is to summarize where we are with regard to our current negotiations under the U.S.-Japan framework. As you know, Ambassador Kantor is in Japan right now, and he is making maximum efforts to push our proposals along.

But I want to tell you from my standpoint where I think we are, making some allowance for anything that may happen in the next 24 hours which I might not be aware of.

There are four principal elements to the U.S. proposal. There are many more, but I think four stand out and, from our standpoint, it is worth focusing on these four which we see as a precondition for successful agreement.

The first is that we are asking the Japanese companies to increase significantly the purchase of parts made in the United States. As you know, there has been a trend over the last couple of years of increasing purchases. We want to see that continue and we would like to see that increase.

Secondly, we have asked the Japanese companies in the U.S. to increase the North American content in their automobiles.

Third, in focusing on the Japanese market itself and the market for sales of U.S. vehicles, we have been focusing on an expansion of dual-franchise dealerships in Japan, so that the Big Three can have the same opportunity to sell their cars in Japan as Japanese car-makers have in the U.S.

Fourth, we are asking the Japanese government to move swiftly to deregulate and simplify procedures that concern imported cars, particularly procedures relating to inspection and certification.

I might add that we also feel that the Japanese government can help to expand the after-market for parts, which we also consider to be quite important. I might add that we are also focusing on strong enforcement of the antitrust laws in Japan.

In most of these areas, in the purchase of parts made in the U.S., in the question of North American content, when it comes to dual-franchise dealerships, we are intent on having quantitative criteria so that we can measure progress.

As you mentioned, we have a counterproposal from Japan which goes in a different direction. The thrust of the Japanese proposal is to look back after a certain number of years and trace what has happened in the automotive trade, and then decide whether or not that constitutes progress. The Japanese proposal entails more studies and does not come to grips with what we consider to be the spirit and the letter of the framework agreement as it relates to measuring progress.

I would like to just review with you the efforts that we have made, to make sure that we are in close touch with the auto companies and the parts companies, and that our negotiating position is based to the maximum extent on efforts to understand this industry.

In the short time since I have been confirmed, I personally have met with the Auto Parts Advisory Committee on more than one occasion, with representatives of the major parts trade associations, with representatives of the UAW, and I have talked at length with the presidents of individual parts companies. I have gone to Detroit, I have met with senior executives from each of the Big Three, and I have also met with their Washington representatives here. I have met with individual members of Congress, and I have had the pleasure of addressing and discussing these issues with the Northeast-Midwest Congressional Coalition.

In Japan, I have talked directly to the top executives of the major automobile companies, I have met with the senior executives of the parts association, the dealers association, and the Japanese Automobile Association. In my view, the administration has done as much as it possibly can to understand the situation.

Turning to the current status, it is fair to say that at this point, barring anything that has happened in the last 12 hours, we have no agreement on any points of our proposal with Japan. We have a disagreement, in fact, about the purpose of the framework, let alone the details of our proposal. It will not come as a surprise that the Japanese counterproposal is totally unacceptable to us, since it does not focus on the future and does not entail procedures for measuring progress.

Until last week, we believed that many people in the Japanese government were focused not on the framework talks, but on issues of reform. We were pleased that the Prime Minister was able to get a reform package through the legislature, and we are hopeful that this will mean much more intensive attention to our proposals. As I mentioned, Ambassador Kantor is there now and he is doing everything he can to push this along.

Let me make one final comment, and that is that, in the event that we are not able to reach agreement by the summit, we do not intend to paper over what is a non-agreement. These are very serious issues, this is one of the top trade priorities for the Clinton administration. As you mentioned, we are intent on opening markets abroad, and there will be no let-up in this process.

Thank you, Mr. Chairman.

Senator LEVIN. Thank you, Mr. Garten. We appreciate your efforts here.

First, how does Japan's keiretsu system restrict our products and discriminate against our auto parts? Can you explain that simply?

Mr. GARTEN. Well, the word "keiretsu" means a lot of different things to different people. I think to oversimplify, the industrial structure of Japan, the industrial and financial structure is much tighter than it is in our country and perhaps in any other country.

The notion of antitrust has no history in Japan, except since the Second World War, when provisions in the Japanese Constitution for antitrust were basically inserted by the American occupation authorities.

In the early days of our trade negotiations with Japan, we focused on tariffs and quotas. But once many of those were eliminated, we saw another kind of *de facto* trade barrier, the industrial structure itself, which is so concentrated that it has been highly resistant to imports, not just of auto parts, but of virtually all manufactured goods.

Senator LEVIN. Not just imports, but the competition, is that fair to say?

Mr. GARTEN. Well, as you know, I lived in Japan for 3 years——

Senator LEVIN. I mean from our auto parts.

Mr. GARTEN. From our auto parts.

Senator LEVIN. The bottom line is are we allowed to fairly compete for that market?

Mr. GARTEN. In my view, no.

Senator LEVIN. Now, since we are not allowed to fairly compete for that market, are we going to place equivalent restrictions on their products, equivalent to the type of restrictions that they place on our products? When will we do that finally?

Mr. GARTEN. As you know, our——

Senator LEVIN. I'm talking about auto parts. I know we have done it in one or two other areas and it has done some good, by the way, apparently in a couple other areas. But when are we going to finally do it in the biggest part of this trade deficit with Japan, in the auto area? If we cannot fairly compete in the auto parts area, when are we finally going to decide we are going to place restrictions on their products equivalent to the restrictions on our auto parts? When will it be—this year? Next year? Give me an estimate. We have been waiting 25 years.

Mr. GARTEN. Do you want a quantitative answer?

Senator LEVIN. Just an estimate of when will we do it. I just need a date.

Mr. GARTEN. I do not have a date. To be honest, I do not know whether that would be one of the measures that we would take. I do not rule it out. I do not rule anything out, but our sole objective——

Senator LEVIN. Let me get to the real point here. Do we know what actions we will take, if we fail to open up that market in a reasonable agreement? Will we know that in advance of the summit?

Mr. GARTEN. Well, we have everything under review. My feeling is, in the first instance, we still intend to succeed. The history of these kinds of negotiations is that when they succeed, a lot happens in the last few days, so I do not want to give the impression that just because are very far apart now, we will not have an agreement by the summit. But it is the case that we have all options under review, as we should, including——

Senator LEVIN. Including the option I have outlined?

Mr. GARTEN. Well, I would rather not get into——

Senator LEVIN. You said all options. I just want to know whether that is one of the options under review.

Mr. GARTEN. I cannot answer that.

Senator LEVIN. Whatever option we choose, will we notify the Japanese as to what action we will take in the event that negotiations fail and notify them in advance or at least during the negotiations?

Mr. GARTEN. Senator, I will ask you to appreciate that we are in the last stages of a very tough and very delicate negotiation, and I would rather not discuss exactly what our strategy is going to be in these last couple of days.

Senator LEVIN. I am not asking you what action we will take.

Mr. GARTEN. I know.

Senator LEVIN. I am simply asking will we let them know either before or during negotiations what actions we will take in the event that negotiations fail?

Mr. GARTEN. I would prefer not to answer that question now.

Senator LEVIN. Let me simply say, again, that unless we are willing to do that, number one, negotiations will fail. I do not see how you possibly can achieve an outcome that is reasonable to open up a market, unless you inform the other side of what will happen if negotiations fail. So I will state, as my urging of the Administration, that whatever action we are going to take in the event of failure of negotiations, that we decide that in advance and inform them in advance.

Otherwise, it seems to me they are dealing with a completely unknown quantity, and that is what they have been dealing with for 25 years, and that is why those deficits continue to rise. While we have been yakking for a decade, called the MOSS talks, that is what has happened to the auto parts deficit. It has gone up dramatically.

Let me ask you, now, about the figures, because there has been a lot of confusion about these figures, Mr. Garten. There was an agreement that Japan would seek to achieve $19 billion in the purchase of U.S. parts. That was an agreement which Prime Minister Miyazawa and President Bush agreed to, I believe, in 1992, is that correct? And that $19 billion figure was for 1994?

Mr. GARTEN. Yes, and that included both purchases in the U.S. and exports from the U.S.

Senator LEVIN. Now, as I understand that figure—I would like to work through this with you—that was projected to be $4 billion in exports to Japan and approximately $15 billion in auto parts which would be used here. Is that correct?

Mr. GARTEN. That is my understanding, yes.

Senator LEVIN. I want to focus now on that $15 billion. that includes parts which are sold to Japanese transplants by U.S.-owned supplier companies, as well as by the Japanese-affiliated parts companies in the United States, is that correct?

Mr. GARTEN. Yes.

Senator LEVIN. As a matter of fact, I believe most of that would come from the Japanese-affiliated parts companies in the United States. Do we know that?

Mr. GARTEN. Right.

Senator LEVIN. In any event, a significant part of it. It is that part that I want to focus on particularly. Am I correct in stating that in terms of the source of those components that come from the Japanese-affiliated parts companies, that a significant percentage of those components in turn come from Japan?

Mr. GARTEN. Yes.

Senator LEVIN. So that when we say, for instance, that they have made a commitment of $19 billion in the purchase of U.S. parts, that is not $19 billion in parts that are sourced and made in the U.S., is that correct?

Mr. GARTEN. That is correct.

Senator LEVIN. That is a very important point. We have been unable, you have been unable, we have been unable to get from the Japanese what the source is of the parts that they call U.S., is that correct?

Mr. GARTEN. Well, we——

Senator LEVIN. We cannot get the dollar breakdown as to that?

Mr. GARTEN. That is right.

Senator LEVIN. We know that a significant part—we will find out later today one study about this—a significant part of the components that are sold here to Japanese transplant assembly plants and which come from particularly Japanese affiliated parts plants are, in turn, sourced in Japan. Is that correct?

Mr. GARTEN. That is correct.

Senator LEVIN. We are not talking here of a small percentage, by the way. I do not know if you want to estimate that percentage or not. Is it fair to say it is a significant percentage?

Mr. GARTEN. That is fair. Let me just check if we have an estimate. I do not know. No, we do not have an estimate.

Senator LEVIN. Let me go through a chart with you, if you would. I do not know if you can read that. Can you see those numbers? Why don't we give Mr. Garten a copy of that chart.

This is a 1992 study made by the Economic Strategy Institute of a 1991 Honda Accord. I assume there are some changes since then.

Here are the estimates. Now, this is what the claim is. The claim is that the North American parts, the claimed U.S. parts—do you see that line, claimed U.S. parts?

Mr. GARTEN. Yes.

Senator LEVIN [continuing]. In that automobile were $200, and the imported parts from Japan were $3,820. Those are the two figures in the column called total. That is what the claim was, imported parts from Japan $3,820—do you see that up there?

Mr. GARTEN. Yes.

Senator LEVIN. [continuing]. And claimed U.S. parts, $4,210. Are you with me so far, Mr. Garten?

Mr. GARTEN. Yes.

Senator LEVIN. Now, the claimed U.S. parts figure is based on the following: That $4,210 figure is based on the following two figures, and this is what the claim is: U.S.-owned supplier parts,

$1,585, and parts supplied by Japanese-affiliated parts companies in the United States, $2,625. Do you see those two figures?

Mr. GARTEN. Yes.

Senator LEVIN. Then you put those two together and that comes up to $4,200. Therefore, the claim is that a majority of that Honda Accord was U.S. parts.

Now let me show you the facts according to the Economic Strategy Institute. The facts are, according to this study, that of the $2,625, which were claimed to be U.S. parts, that two-thirds of those parts in fact were sourced in Japan. Do you follow what I am saying now on that chart?

Mr. GARTEN. Yes, I do.

Senator LEVIN. Of the $2,625 which was listed as part of the U.S. parts, that two-thirds of that in fact was Japan-sourced, and the specific figures were $1,775 Japan sourced, and $850 North American sourced. So instead of the majority of that car that year being in fact U.S.-made parts—and that is what the claim was, $4,200 compared to imported parts of $3,800—when you total the actual source of the parts, that it was $5,600 Japan sourced and $2,435 U.S. or North American sourced.

Now, I do not know whether you are familiar with this study or not, but would you not agree that in order to have any accurate estimate of what the true U.S. content is of components, that we have got to see the source of those components? Because most of the components come from Japan and the majority of the components are simply assembled here by a parts supplier and then sent to a transplant assembly plant, that that gives a distorted figure as to what the true U.S. content is. Would you agree with that?

Mr. GARTEN. I would just like to make one or two comments on this, if I could.

Senator LEVIN. Surely.

Mr. GARTEN. I came to Washington after this study was done, and I was not around when it came out, so I hesitate to give it any credibility, without myself knowing what the underlying assumptions are, which are obviously critical.

Senator LEVIN. Right.

Mr. GARTEN. But what comes to my mind is that the starting point of looking at something like this—well, there are a couple of starting points. One is what you are saying, that claims have to be examined very carefully and disaggregated, so that you really know where the parts are coming from. Of course, I agree with that.

Senator LEVIN. We do not have that information.

Mr. GARTEN. We do not have that information. The second, though, is I think we have to be aware that this is a truly global industry and that any study at any given time—it is not only a global industry, but it is a very dynamic one—any study at any given time is likely to be years out of date.

I think that the way to deal with this, which I presume is where you are leading to, is that we need better information, and we have been asking the Japanese——

Senator LEVIN. We have or have not?

Mr. GARTEN. We need better information in order to understand this phenomenon. We have on the one hand asked the Japanese Automobile Association, which has supplied a lot of this, to disaggregate their figures, which they do not do, and we also have built into our proposal a provision to have third-party auditing so that we get a better handle on this.

Senator LEVIN. On this exact issue?

Mr. GARTEN. On this issue and on all of the measurable issues.

Senator LEVIN. But this is one of the measurable issues.

Mr. GARTEN. This is one of them and this is major. I do not want to say anything else. What I want to say is it is not just a question of a study. We need a system and——

Senator LEVIN. Because we do not have a system, we are doing the best we can, is that right?

Mr. GARTEN. Right. The other thing, though, is that in our proposal we are asking the Japanese auto companies to reach levels of North American content that are significantly high, so that a lot of this problem goes away.

In measuring that local content, that North American content, we want to use at least three different systems. We want to use the CAFE standards, we want to use the NAFTA standards which provide for a good deal of tracing back, so that you know where the parts originated from, and we want to use the standards of the upcoming American Automobile Labeling Act, which sets the threshold of local content high enough so that many of these problems will be quite visible, because with that Automobile Labeling Act you will know that an American car will have to have 70 percent local content, and it is a black and white question.

Senator LEVIN. Defined how?

Mr. GARTEN. By parts that are made in the U.S.

Senator LEVIN. Made, not bought?

Mr. GARTEN. Made.

Senator LEVIN. Is that correct?

Mr. GARTEN. Made in the U.S.

Senator LEVIN. Not bought in the U.S.?

Mr. GARTEN. Made in the U.S., or made in North America.

Senator LEVIN. Would you agree that there is a critical difference——

Mr. GARTEN. Of course.

Senator LEVIN [continuing]. Between saying parts bought in the U.S. as U.S. parts, which they are not, and parts that are made in the U.S. or made in North America are in fact——

Mr. GARTEN. Analytically, it is a benchmark, it is——

Senator LEVIN. Do not get too analytical. Jobs is a big difference.

Mr. GARTEN. OK.

Senator LEVIN. Do you not agree?

Mr. GARTEN. Yes. The point I want to make is this, that we are aware of the statistical problem, and we are attempting to deal with this as best we can. I think it would be unrealistic, however, in such a dynamic global industry, to think that we will ever have as good a handle on what is being bought from where as you would obviously like.

Senator LEVIN. But we could have a lot better handle than we have been given by the Japanese so far, can we not? It is a pretty obvious reason why we are not given that information, by the way, because the figures come out totally different. By those figures, the majority of the parts in that vehicle are claimed to be U.S. parts.

That is what they claim. Whereas, the best facts we can get, because we cannot get better facts from the Japanese, is that the vast majority of the parts in that vehicle in fact are Japan sourced, more than two-thirds.

Now that is something which we ought not gloss over in any way. That is a very major difference. I have to tell you what particularly galls me is that the same folks who refuse to give us the data so that we can make this kind of assessment, now claim that we should not use the fact that we have some parts coming from Japanese-owned or Japanese-affiliated companies any differently than American-owned companies. By the way, the only reason you have got to do that is because they will not give you the data.

I happen to think that it is not the best way to go. Ownership is not the best way to go. I happen to agree with that. But these are the folks who will not give us the data so we get a better measure. You know, we get a JAMA news release today saying we should not look at ownership. What the heck difference does ownership make? The only reason you look at that is because it becomes the only available measure.

We know the Japanese-affiliated parts companies purchase many of the parts going into a component from Japan. We know that U.S.-owned companies do that far less. So we use that as the metaphor; we use that as the best thing we have got available, and then they complain that we are using the ownership issue, when they will not give us the data. Give us the data, folks. JAMA is out there, I know. We got press releases put on our table this morning. JAMA, give us the data, wherever you are and whoever you are, and then we will not have to use the U.S.-owned and the Japanese-owned standard.

That is my challenge to you, give us the data. You have not done it in 20 years. We have it as part of NAFTA. We get the sourcing. As Mr. Garten just mentioned, that is one of the ways we are seeking now in these negotiations. You cannot have it both ways. You cannot argue against using the ownership and then refuse to give us a better measure, the most accurate measure, which is the source of the parts and the components.

I think what we will try to do is invite JAMA here next week to a hearing, by the way, and we will go into that issue with them, so they do not have to just issue a press release. They can come here and State their case. We will not invite you back, because I know you are going to be part of the summit negotiations next week.

This is my final question, Mr. Garten. The U.S. and Japan have conducted a study of Japan's distribution system of autos and auto parts. The study was a joint study conducted by the U.S. Department of Commerce and MITI. I understand that the study found that Japan's distribution system discriminated against foreign autos. Could you give us the status of that study and why it has not been released?

Mr. GARTEN. We wanted to release the study about 2 weeks ago, and the Japanese Government asked for some more time because of what they called "translation problems." We have been talking to them and urging that we jointly release the study, which was the understanding at the beginning, and I am hopeful that we will be able to release it in the next couple of days. I think we are over the translation problems —that is what we heard yesterday—and at a minimum, we should be able to release the executive summary. It is certainly our hope to do so.

Senator LEVIN. Why just the executive summary?

Mr. GARTEN. I think there is a production problem in terms of the major study is very thick. We will release what we can logistically do.

Senator LEVIN. How thick is the major study?

Mr. GARTEN. I gather it is over 300 pages, and the agreement was it would have to be released both in English and in Japanese.

Senator LEVIN. I see.

Mr. GARTEN. So the translation logistics apparently are quite difficult.

Senator LEVIN. I thought you said the translation now has been overcome.

Mr. GARTEN. The translation on the executive summary.

Senator LEVIN. Just on the executive summary.

Mr. GARTEN. Yes.

Senator LEVIN. I am afraid this is typical. Do not let them wear you out. They have not worn us out. Twenty-five years, and they still have not worn us out. We are going to continue to press this issue until it is finally resolved. We know our auto parts are competitive by every other measure—take a look at the EC, take a look at Mexico, take a look at Canada. We either have a surplus in auto parts, or we are even in auto parts with the rest of the world. But when you take a look at our auto parts trade with Japan, it is 10 to 1 with respect to imports and exports. And that is true not just against us, but against every other country.

So we will look forward to the complete study before the summit, and we would appreciate your answering questions that some of my colleagues may have for you for the record.

Mr. GARTEN. I would be delighted.

Senator LEVIN. We wish you well. Thanks so much for being here.

Mr. GARTEN. I thank you very much for the opportunity.

Senator LEVIN. Our next panel is made up of two people, and we are happy to welcome them here. Mr. Robert Cole is vice president of government affairs at Kaiser Aluminum and Chemical Corporation, and also chairman of the Annual Report Task Force of APAC, the Auto Parts Advisory Committee that advises the administration on auto parts negotiations with Japan.

And our other witness on this panel is Dr. Michael Flynn, who is associate director of the Office for the Study of Automotive Transportation at the University of Michigan.

We welcome you both, and Mr. Cole, could you begin, and summarize your testimony if you would, so we can have time for questions? Your entire testimony will be made part of the record.

TESTIMONY OF ROBERT E. COLE,[1] VICE PRESIDENT, GOVERNMENT AFFAIRS, KAISER ALUMINUM AND CHEMICAL CORPORATION, AND CHAIRMAN, ANNUAL REPORT TASK FORCE, AUTO PARTS ADVISORY COMMITTEE

Mr. COLE. I would be glad to, Mr. Chairman. Thank you.

I appreciate the opportunity to present testimony today on APAC's 1993 report, "U.S.-Japan Auto Parts Trade Five Years after the Fair Trade in Auto Parts Act: A Results-Oriented Review." The report is also being submitted to the Subcommittee.

I also appreciate the support, Mr. Chairman, that you have given in terms of support for the auto parts industry and our objectives in competing in a fair and open marketplace in the United States and in Japan.

APAC members are very pleased that the automotive industries, including both the motor vehicle and the auto parts sectors, have been designated as major sectors under the Framework negotiations, and that the United States Government has presented to the Japanese a comprehensive proposal on autos and auto parts that focuses on three main areas—purchases of U.S. auto parts by Japanese transplant vehicle manufactures; purchases of foreign auto parts in Japan; and imports of foreign vehicles by Japan.

The achievement of the U.S. objectives in the Framework negotiations is very important to the success of the Clinton administration's programs for revitalization of the domestic economy in the United States, for expanding U.S. exports, and for guiding the post-Cold War transition of persons employed in the military and defense industries to civilian employment.

The U.S. proposal we think should also be compatible with the Japanese Government's objectives of political and regulatory reform and transforming of the export-oriented Japanese economy to a more consumer-oriented economy.

The motor vehicle and auto parts industries are essential to the health of the American economy. The data that you presented in your excellent opening statement and the data which Mr. Flynn is going to present certainly support that conclusion, so I will not go into the details there.

I will say that no other economic sectors in the United States have anywhere near the potential of the motor vehicle and the auto parts industries to grow through increased exports and through displacement of imports to accomplish the domestic economic recovery and defense conversion goals of the Clinton administration and the Congress.

Exports of U.S. auto parts have grown substantially since 1988, accounting for approximately $33.1 billion in U.S. exports in 1993. Since 1989, the United States would have run an overall trade surplus in auto parts each year, except for the large trade deficit with Japan. The deficit with Japan was $11 billion in 1993, compared with $8.8 billion in 1988.

Studies for APAC have projected that the auto parts deficit with Japan will likely remain at current very high levels or worsen during the next several years. The trade deficits with Japan and accompanying economic dislocations in the United States are persist-

[1] The prepared statement of Mr. Cole appears on page 44.

ent despite dramatic and well-documented improvements in the competitiveness of the American auto parts industry, and despite American industry leadership in the newest high-technology areas, such as airbags, antilock brake systems, and light-weight materials.

The trade deficit is growing despite dramatic changes in the yen-dollar ratios in recent years, which have favored U.S.-manufactured products.

The American Government and industry have conducted numerous studies of the competitiveness of the U.S. auto parts industry and of the barriers to trade with the Japanese. Those are documented in a series of reports that APAC has issued and included this year in a bibliography for our 1993 report.

The problems confronted by traditional U.S. manufacturers are numerous and thus well-documented. Since 1988, the United States and Japanese also have conducted a variety of bilateral trade negotiations—MOSS, MOCP, SII, and now the Framework Agreement.

A significant advance in the efforts to increase trade in auto parts occurred in January of 1992, when the Japanese commitments were announced for the Global Partnership and the Global Partnership Plan of Action. The Plan of Action included descriptions of the Japanese car companies' "voluntary purchase plans" for buying $19 billion in U.S. auto parts in 1994.

Your comments earlier today, Mr. Chairman, also brought out a number of the difficulties in understanding fully what that commitment means and how it will be implemented vis-a-vis American suppliers and American-made products.

Two years have passed since the Japanese Government and the vehicle manufactures announced their voluntary plans for fiscal year 94. No such announcements have been made for fiscal year 95 or fiscal year 96, nor have other significant achievements been made in bilateral auto parts negotiations with Japan in the last 2 years.

Kaiser Aluminum is implementing comprehensive programs to substantially expand business with the Japanese vehicle industry. Kaiser has an office in Tokyo, Japan. Kaiser has formed a Tokyo-based joint venture company with Furukawa Electric Company and Itochu Corporation, to serve the Japanese ground transportation industry and other selected Asian markets.

Kaiser also has an agreement with Furukawa, Kawasaki Steel Corporation, and Pechiney, to develop aluminum body sheet for the automotive market. Several Kaiser business units are working directly with Japanese companies, including Toyota, Mazda, and Honda, on possible business. Kaiser has had extensive and cordial business discussions with the Japanese companies, and some of our facilities and our products have been extensively evaluated.

Unfortunately, Kaiser's activities to date have not resulted in any firm business for either Kaiser directly or our Tokyo-based joint venture company. However, we remain committed; we know we are competitive, and we are determined to be successful.

Like others in the U.S. auto parts industry we at Kaiser are anxiously watching the Framework negotiations and sincerely hoping they will be successful. APAC has made extensive and cohesive policy recommendations to the Secretary of Commerce for actions to increase trade with Japan in the U.S. and in the Japanese domestic markets. APAC's policies reflect strong support for open markets for motor vehicles and auto parts, in which success is achievable through fair and open competition among manufacturers.

APAC members are confident that the U.S. auto parts industry can successfully compete in every automotive market in the world if competition is not restricted by nonmarket barriers or exclusionary practices, either imposed or tolerated by national governments.

APAC strongly recommends that prompt removal of such barriers and exclusionary practices must be a major objective of the U.S. Government.

APAC has strongly supported the U.S. Government's position in the Framework negotiations. We seek market-based, reasonable, and measurable results. We urge the Government to continue to insist on achievement of the 1994 Japanese parts purchases and local content targets, with special emphasis on traditional U.S. suppliers.

We have also urged the opening of the original equipment and after-market in Japan to U.S. suppliers and continuous improvements in expanded purchases and design-in relationships with U.S. suppliers in North America in order to reach an equitable and sustainable auto parts trade relationship with Japan by 1988.

Achieving major annual reductions in the massive and growing U.S. auto parts deficit with Japan is also essential and should be accomplished over a five-year period to a level which reflects U.S. industry's strong international competitive position.

Monitoring the progress which non-Japanese-affiliated U.S. automotive suppliers are making with the Japanese companies in Japan and in the United States is also important to judge how fast we are achieving our goals.

APAC has supported a Clinton administration review of the options for U.S. actions, including U.S. Government self-initiation of trade actions such as anti-dumping, section 301, and the proposed Super 301 extension, against any country, including Japan, which does not live up to its fair trade obligations as a major participant in the global auto parts market.

APAC also supports extension of the Fair Trade in Auto Parts Act, which was requested of Congress by the Clinton administration last year, and which you have introduced as legislation.

The United States Government's trade efforts must be persistent, and the close industry-Government cooperation, which has been extremely strong since the establishment of APAC, must continue if the U.S. Government and the U.S. auto parts industry are to achieve their mutual objectives for economic growth, high-quality employment, competition-based business opportunities, and leading-edge technological advances that historically have provided enormous benefits to the American people in our consumer-oriented economy.

Thank you, Mr. Chairman.

Senator LEVIN. Thank you, Mr. Cole.

Dr. Flynn, a particular welcome to you after that great basketball victory the other night.

TESTIMONY OF MICHAEL S. FLYNN,[1] ASSOCIATE DIRECTOR, OFFICE FOR THE STUDY OF AUTOMOTIVE TRANSPORTATION, UNIVERSITY OF MICHIGAN TRANSPORTATION RESEARCH INSTITUTE

Mr. FLYNN. Thank you, Senator. I have submitted a written statement, so I am going to try to summarize.

Senator LEVIN. Thank you.

Mr. FLYNN. I would like to touch on three topics: the importance and likely future developments in the bilateral automotive trade balance, particularly in light of some recent competitive developments; second, the level of economic activity in the automotive supplier sector that is generated by vehicle assembly and how might it differ between the Japanese-affiliated and traditional U.S. assembly operations; and third, I want to address the issue, which I must say was hotter than I expected it to be, of how do you objectively try to measure the U.S. supplier content of vehicles so that we can determine a baseline for assessing change.

I should say at the outset that I find one of the basic premises of the Framework negotiations very promising. As I understand it, the Framework hopes to develop reasonable measures of the current situation so that both Japan and the United States are addressing the issue from a common understanding if not a shared perspective.

Such a jointly recognized measure would, I believe, permit more fruitful and beneficial negotiations as to progress in deficit reduction, selection of methods to reduce that deficit, and a common frame of reference for resolving outstanding issues.

I must say I am somewhat disheartened that so much of the public debate has so far degenerated to disputes about targets, goals and pledges, and about which country now adheres more closely to free trade principles.

I think, as the Under Secretary pointed out, with the increasing globalization and internationalization of the industry, it is getting harder and harder to lump all the Japanese companies, or for that matter, all the American companies. It is certainly my impression that the Japanese companies in North America have quite different sourcing patterns in terms of domestic versus import content as well as contained import content through Japanese-affiliated suppliers.

It is also my impression from talking to suppliers over the last few years that there are differences in the seriousness with which the Japanese companies are attempting to increase U.S. sourcing, and I do think we need to recognize that.

Whether they are doing this for reasons of reducing friction, or because of the clear performance advantages that the U.S. supplier industry is developing I think is moot, but it is the case that some do appear to be much more successful, at least, in signing contracts than others.

I am not going to review the overall parts trade deficit except to note that one of the reasons I will not do it is that our work has all been based on ITC data, and one of the problems we have in this area is not just the difference between JAMA data and U.S.

[1] The prepared statement of Mr. Flynn appears on page 101.

Government data, but the difference within the U.S. Government between ITC and DOC data. So I will skip that for fear that I would simply wind up confusing the issue.

I would like to jump ahead to the issue of where is that deficit, however measured, in whatever specificity, and with whatever dataset, going. In particular, there has been some suggestion that perhaps these negotiations may not be as important, because after all, the Big Three are doing so well.

No question the news out of Detroit is good. The Big Three gained about two points of production share in the 1993 vehicle market. Their profit performance is improving, in some cases quite dramatically. They appear to have substantially reduced the quality advantages of the Japanese nameplates, and now even enjoy a price advantage over comparable Japanese vehicles.

The market continues to shift to light trucks, a segment of our market in which the Big Three enjoy a share of over 86 percent as opposed to their more modest share of 60 percent or so of the car market.

From a national perspective, there is the added good news of a continued increase in the share of Japanese nameplate sales that are sourced here in the United States or in Canada rather than in Japan.

All of that looks very good, but what I want to stress is that the return of better times to Detroit, and the increased reliance on North American-sourced vehicles by the Japanese manufacturers in and of themselves will not eliminate the National problem of that troublesome deficit.

We did trade projections last year based on data through 1992 that reflect exactly what is now developing in the market. We assumed that the light truck share of the market would go up; we assumed that the Japanese would lose sales share in the market. We did some very optimistic scenarios of U.S. exports, and what we find is that, depending on the size of the market, and what exactly happens with Japanese share, that in fact, the total deficit in 1996 is likely to swing around the value of its 1992 level. It could easily, in a strong market, with stable Japanese share, grow by 11 percent, although that would be less, I should stress, than the market would grow. In an average market with declining market share, we could even look forward to a decline in the deficit of as much as 10 percent.

Underlying this is a continued strong importance of the parts trade as a source of the deficit. The basic composition of the deficit changed dramatically in the 1980's with the opening of Japanese-affiliated manufacturing operations in the United States, and that change remains with us and appears unlikely to go away.

Japanese transplant, as they are called, sourcing is going to be a major driver of the deficit because it will be a major driver of sourcing of Japanese parts.

I do want to stress that there are estimates that differ quite radically with the chart you showed earlier. Our analysis suggests that as of 1992, we could associate with the average transplant or new entrant or Japanese-affiliated, whatever your preference, vehicle about $3,300, $3,345, actually, in imported content.

That was a rise from an earlier study we did, an increase of about $300, although in our view, inflation and the enriched Japanese product mix in their North American assembly operations suggests that in absolute terms it has declined.

That is an extremely high level of import content, and it seems to me that from a national perspective, that is what we need to focus on. We have done work in a number of areas looking at the issue of what is the domestic sourcing of the Japanese-affiliated assemblers, and in fact, I believe the chart that was shown here begins with our data. I should stress that the claimed Japanese content, the claimed U.S. parts—that was our claim; that was not Honda's claim. This is not something that Honda ever put out and said, "Look at what we are doing." This is what the University of Michigan put out and said this was our estimate of the U.S. parts in a domestically assembled Accord.

The Economic Strategy Institute then took those results, and they made the estimate of how much of the total was actually sourced in the United States and how much was imported, so that there is a fairly long chain of activity underlying that graph. I think it reinforces the Under Secretary's point that things are changing in some cases so rapidly that we do need a system rather than a study if we are going to——

Senator LEVIN. Just while you are on that point, the $4,210 figure includes the $2,625 that were supplied by the Japanese-affiliated parts companies.

Mr. FLYNN. Yes.

Senator LEVIN. And did you break down the $2,625 as to their source?

Mr. FLYNN. No, we did not.

Senator LEVIN. That is what the Economic Strategy Institute did.

Mr. FLYNN. That is what the Economic Strategy Institute did.

Senator LEVIN. And do you agree or disagree with that breakdown?

Mr. FLYNN. I do not know the details of their methodology, so I really cannot comment. The result does not surprise me. To the extent that I would guess, it is sort of in the ballpark of what I would have guessed at that time.

There are some disturbing patterns in the data that JAMA has released that I think bear a special comment. In our earlier 1991 trade study, we noticed that through 1991 there was a curious pattern in the development of bilateral exports in the automotive sector. High-value exports were the fast-growing Japanese exports to the U.S. Lower-value were the fast-growing U.S. exports to Japan. There is an imbalance there that seems to show up as well in the JAMA data. If we look at the JAMA-MITI data on total U.S. purchases versus our trade data, there is a suggestion that the higher-value, more strictly defined automotive goods, the more technically sophisticated goods that are being purchased by the Japanese have become a lower portion of their total buy in the U.S., falling from 51 percent in 1986 to 40 percent in 1991.

I think it also bears mention—and it is in the written testimony—that the location of engineering is quite different for the two industries.

I want to make a couple of additional comments, and then I will cease, on the measurement of U.S. content. I strongly, strongly believe that a lot of the arguments that we are hearing do have to do with different definitions and different measures and different measurement procedures and different treatment of the data. I think there is a fundamental difference in how we look at the problem; we want to look ahead to when the problem is eliminated. And the Japanese want to look back and say, "But we are making progress," at least by some numbers, in that direction.

But I think it is very important to recognize that one of the reasons that the data that has been adduced so far, whether in our trade study or in the JAMA-MITI, is so problematic is that it is rife with measurement problems. There are definitional issues. There is undoubtedly double-counting going on in the JAMA data of domestic purchases and exports. We buy steel for domestic use and making in fact a part that is exported to Japan, and that is going to be counted twice—as it would be if it were GM or Chrysler or Ford making the report.

Some of the Japanese companies have told us they do include in their reports non-U.S., but U.S. company purchases. So a GM part bought from a GM facility in Europe shows up in those data as a U.S. purchase. I think there is a standard problem that CAFE has given us. CAFE only counts the origin of the part, basically in terms of the mailing address. You do not have to tighten the screws, Senator, to have it count as CAFE. The most you have to do is let it sit in your warehouse long enough for the "value" to change, which probably is about 2 minutes, and ship it on, and for CAFE purposes, it becomes U.S. content.

That whole psychology of "imports to the suppliers do not matter," I think is a problem in addressing this issue.

And finally, there are double-counts when materials are included in parts. I buy steel, I make a component, I sell to my assembly plant. The way the books are kept, that is almost inevitably going to be counted twice.

I stress—all of those are correctable, and if we correct them, then I do believe the approach that JAMA and MITI are taking, with a broader measurement of what constitutes an automotive good, makes sense. What they are stressing is that if Toyota buys a part, or a piece of raw material, or anything, and sends it to Japan or uses it domestically in automotive production, it is an auto good. Our trade data defines that much more restrictively, and the steel or aluminum that Honda might buy here and ship to Japan would not show up as part of the automotive analysis; that is probably a mistake.

I do want to, however, depart with my agreement with most of the Under Secretary's remarks, and say please, please, do not give us three more sets of measures. It seems to me that a broad-based automotive measure, one that includes the NAFTA tracing requirements, will meet any of the needs that I can foresee in measuring progress in getting good, accurate, agreed-to data, getting data that can be audited and so forth. That will be met very nicely by a NAFTA-type determination with a tracing requirement. It will not be met by CAFE nor do I think it will be met by labelling, because that excludes assembly, and to me that makes very little sense if you are in fact trying to determine the entire automotive situation.

With that, I will end. Thank you.

Senator LEVIN. Thank you very much, Dr. Flynn.

First of all, Mr. Cole, let me mention to you about the reauthorization of the Auto Parts Advisory Committee issue. I was able to get that reauthorization added to the State Department Authorization Bill which just passed yesterday.

Mr. COLE. We appreciate that very much. That is very good news.

Senator LEVIN. You should be aware, then, of the fact that on that bill leaving the Senate, we got the 5-year reauthorization, and now we have got to work on the House to see that it stays on the State Department Authorization Bill. So I am sure you will be helpful in that.

Mr. COLE. We will do everything we can to make sure that happens.

Senator LEVIN. Just to let you know that I was able to add it to this bill.

Mr. COLE. Thank you.

Senator LEVIN. Are you optimistic that the results-oriented approach, Mr. Cole, is going to get any better results than we have had before?

Mr. COLE. At this point, it is very hard to be optimistic. Both the Japanese Government and JAMA, as you know, have been very critical of the U.S. Government's position. And taking their views at face value, it is very difficult for us to think that there is going to be a major breakthrough late in the process, even though we know as these trade negotiations normally occur, breakthroughs do not happen until the last minute. But I know of no reason to be optimistic today.

Senator LEVIN. The Japanese Government and the auto manufacturers have responded to our pressure to open markets by saying that the markets are open, and that the reason foreign auto parts make up less than 2 percent of Japan's total auto parts market is because U.S. industry has not tried hard enough and that the quality of our parts is not as high as theirs.

Number one, what is your response to that, and number two, how could that make any sense given the fact that we have a surplus with the rest of the world?

Mr. COLE. I think the fact that we have a surplus with the rest of the world and the data for the rest of the world, as your chart here shows, indicates that there are large flows of auto parts across all borders in both directions, except in Japan, where the flow is only from inside out and not outside in, would indicate that the Japanese market is not in fact open.

I would say that as far as Kaiser is concerned, I took my first trade mission to Japan in 1985, back at the beginning of your chart here, when the problem was a lot less serious than it is today. Kaiser has sent numerous, numerous executives and technical people to Japan in our efforts to seek more business. It has been a decade now. We are making some progress, but progress is very, very slow.

I am sympathetic to the Japanese situation right now, relative to their recession. I would say, however, that in open markets when you have a recession, normally following the recession is a good opportunity to open up to new suppliers. That is what has happened in the United States in the past because U.S. companies have taken the opportunity of difficulty economic times to pick their best suppliers, and it is growth with the new suppliers and with the best suppliers that occurs when the market recovers.

I think it is very important that that also occur in Japan as they end their recession, and their business starts growing again. An open market I believe would reflect that trend.

Senator LEVIN. Are we able to trace the content of a component that comes from a Japanese-affiliated parts company here with any certainty right now? I mean, do we have the information so we can trace it?

Mr. COLE. I am not aware of any studies that have the information. I would say, however, though, that with the computer sophistication of tracking of information nowadays within companies, the computer technicalities are not difficult to work out, and the equipment exists and in fact is used for things like warranties. So, it is not too difficult to work on a system that I think would give the data that is required.

Senator LEVIN. So it is available fairly easily, but not available publicly, you are telling us.

Mr. COLE. I think that is correct, and it would take some massaging, but it should not take years to work the system out.

Senator LEVIN. A recent study said that the U.S. auto industry has a 20 to 30 percent cost advantage over Japanese parts products. Do you have any percentage cost advantage at the moment for equal parts?

Mr. COLE. No, I do not, but those are in the ball park with the numbers I have seen. Of course, it varies by particular product, but we clearly, especially with the yen relationship and with the downsizings and improvements we have made in our own efficiencies, have a significant advantage.

Senator LEVIN. Do you have a job-related figure for each billion dollars of auto parts that are sold either to Japan or that are sold from U.S. parts-makers to the transplants? Do you have an easy figure for us?

Mr. COLE. The figure I tend to use is that every U.S. worker in the automotive industry produces about $100,000 worth of value added, or improvement for business. So I tend to use that. I am probably not the best person to ask because I am not a good statistician. Maybe Mike has a better idea.

Senator LEVIN. I will ask Dr. Flynn that same question, then. Do you have a figure for that, Dr. Flynn?

Mr. FLYNN. We have a couple of them floating through various reports, but I honestly do not remember. The $100,000 figure is a fairly common one. In terms of the automotive supplier, the last one I saw said the value added in the supplier industry is about $70,000 per worker. So in a sense, every $75,000 of imported parts is going to take away a job.

Senator LEVIN. Which would mean that every $750,000 is 10.

Mr. FLYNN. Yes.

Senator LEVIN. I am just trying to figure out how much per billion. Every $7.5 million would then be 100; 1,000 per $75 million—

no, that is too high—10,000 for $750 million. That would mean about 13,000 jobs per billion. Does that sound about right?

Mr. FLYNN. I do not know.

Senator LEVIN. You do not know. OK.

Mr. FLYNN. Senator, I apologize, but I am a sociologist, so I only deal in thousands. Millions and billions are still beyond me.

Senator LEVIN. I am on the Armed Services Committee, so I deal with billions.

Is the Japanese market open now to competition in auto parts, Dr. Flynn?

Mr. FLYNN. I do not believe it is.

Senator LEVIN. I want to go back to that chart just for one minute. Do we have yet available the data from the Japanese companies which would allow us to give a current estimate on the percentage of U.S. content in each car that, for instance, is assembled here by a Japanese transplant? Do we have that data?

Mr. FLYNN. Yes, we have the JAMA data.

Senator LEVIN. No, not the JAMA data. I am talking about the sourcing data of the type that we are going to hopefully get under NAFTA.

Mr. FLYNN. Directly from the companies?

Senator LEVIN. Yes.

Mr. FLYNN. Not to my knowledge.

Senator LEVIN. All right. The NAFTA-type tracing data that you made reference to, you indicated that if we could get that kind of data that that would help this analysis immeasurably; is that right?

Mr. FLYNN. Yes. I really believe that. NAFTA essentially says that if you are going to claim the 62.5 percent North American content for free trade across the southern and northern border, that you will be subject to an audit which requires you to trace that through your suppliers, so that you get around the problem of a supplier who is selling something that is 80 or 90 percent import content. That kind of a part or component would only count as 10 or 20 percent North American content in meeting the NAFTA requirement.

Senator LEVIN. And that is the data we do not now have.

Mr. FLYNN. That is the data that, as far as I am aware, we do not now have.

Senator LEVIN. With Japan?

Mr. FLYNN. With Japan or with anyone else.

Senator LEVIN. And if we could get that with Japan, we could then have a very accurate way of assessing in one common language what percentage of a vehicle is indeed, "U.S. made" and what is Japanese?

Mr. FLYNN. Yes, I believe that.

Senator LEVIN. Are you aware of the claim of some transplants as to a certain percentage of U.S. parts? Have either one of you seen those claims?

Mr. FLYNN. I have.

Senator LEVIN. And as far as you can tell, is that claim based on the counting of 100 percent of the purchase of a part in the U.S. from a Japanese-affiliated company as a U.S. part?

Mr. FLYNN. Oh, yes. Those claims are basically CAFE claims, and that is the problem with them. They are truthful, but the way the CAFE claims are actually calculated, one of the Japanese companies is about to go to EPA to ask that its vehicle be certified domestic. I am quite confident that they believe that they will get the domestic label—and they should if they have reached that content. It is just that that content, the 75 or 80 percent CAFE content, does not translate very directly into import content and trade terms, because of the problem that I have a small shop outside Ann Arbor, Michigan where I buy lots of Japanese and Italian componentry, and I rebadge it and ship it on. And for you, whether you are in Flint, Michigan in a GM assembly plant, or in Marysville, Ohio at Honda, when you receive that part, for CAFE purposes, that is 100 percent domestic.

Senator LEVIN. But for trade purposes——

Mr. FLYNN. For trade purposes, it may be virtually zero percent domestic.

Senator LEVIN. And how about for jobs purposes?

Mr. FLYNN. Well, if it is zero percent domestic content for trade purposes, it is about zero percent for jobs. You know, I have somebody in my factory, maybe stamping, maybe reboxing, maybe a few people, but that is all it would take.

So the claims I have seen from the Japanese companies about their CAFE levels of domestic content generally seem quite credible to me.

Senator LEVIN. In terms of CAFE.

Mr. FLYNN. In terms of CAFE. If you visit the plants, and if you look at the structure of their expenses, yes. In 1991, we thought the Accord, in terms of parts and so on, was in fact up around 62 percent. It was generally reported to be somewhat higher——

Senator LEVIN. Is that CAFE?

Mr. FLYNN. That was sort of the CAFE, not quite. But I had no trouble—at the time, the press was typically reporting 75 percent—I think I would have bet that in terms of true CAFE content, if you did the CAFE calculations, it probably was around 70.

Senator LEVIN. And for trade purposes, jobs purposes?

Mr. FLYNN. Well, for trade purposes, you then get back to either our estimate of imported parts at about $3,300——

Senator LEVIN. So what would that have been—instead of 70 percent, it would have been what, for trade purposes?

Mr. FLYNN. Oh, that would have been based on the total value of the car—about 25 percent, 27, 28 percent.

Senator LEVIN. So in terms of real jobs of U.S. content, it would be 25 percent, not 70 percent?

Mr. FLYNN. That is right.

I am sorry, Senator. I forgot to add in, in fairness to Honda, you have the parts, but you also have the assembly; so it would have been more on the order of 50 percent in terms of jobs.

Senator LEVIN. So in terms of jobs, it would have been 50 instead of 70 or 75.

Mr. FLYNN. Right.

Senator LEVIN. But the main point is we do not have the data to allow us to find that out; is that correct?

Mr. FLYNN. That is right. That is exactly right.

Senator LEVIN. Dr. Flynn, you have written that Japan is reluctant to make high-value, high-wage parts in the United States, such as precision machining and precision casting. A recent University of Michigan study that you authored found that domestic suppliers are generally underrepresented in the three major vehicle systems—engines, transmissions, and body structure—and you found that the areas where the U.S. content suppliers are making inroads in supply to the Japanese include hardware, glass, brakes, wheels tires, and interior hard and soft trim. That was your study.

Mr. FLYNN. That is right.

Senator LEVIN. What is their strategy behind that practice?

Mr. FLYNN. Well, I am not sure what the strategy is. The result is that, if you will, the higher-tech, higher value, more skilled work appears to be remaining in Japan. I should stress that that is not terribly surprising that it would start that way.

I think the real issue is how rapidly does it change, and because we cannot really track those kinds of uses to the different companies, we do not know how fast it is changing. The net impact—the importance of that finding—is that if you think of it in terms of jobs, the better jobs are associated with the work that was still going on in Japan in 1991. The less good jobs in terms of wages and so on was associated with the work that was going on at the U.S. suppliers.

Mr. COLE. I might say, Senator, that it is precisely trying to get into the higher value-added areas that Kaiser and a lot of companies are now trying to focus on.

We have traditionally sold metal to the Japanese companies. We are now trying to sell forged products, extruded products, and other high-technology products, which we have got a good bit of experience in selling to the U.S. companies and outside the automotive field, to the aircraft field, which is very demanding.

We would like to show that capability and get new business with the Japanese in these higher-tech areas.

Senator LEVIN. Thank you both. We appreciate your being here.

Mr. COLE. Thank you.

Mr. FLYNN. Thank you, Senator.

Senator LEVIN. Our last witness is Mr. Andrew Card, who is president and CEO of the American Automobile Manufacturers Association. Mr. Card has just returned from a week in Japan, I believe—I do not know whether you still have jet lag or not——

Mr. CARD. I do, Senator.

Senator LEVIN. [continuing]. And you are going to let us know what your view is on the automotive component of the Framework negotiations.

I am glad you could be with us this morning.

TESTIMONY OF ANDREW H. CARD, JR.,[1] PRESIDENT AND CEO, AMERICAN AUTOMOBILE MANUFACTURERS ASSOCIATION AND FORMER SECRETARY, U.S. DEPARTMENT OF TRANSPORTATION

Mr. CARD. Thank you, Mr. Chairman.

[1] The prepared statement of Mr. Card appears on page 109.

My name is Andrew Card, and I am president and chief executive officer of the American Automobile Manufacturers Association. AAMA is the trade association of America's car companies—Chrysler Corporation, Ford Motor Company, and General Motors Corporation.

Our companies employ more than 730,000 American men and women, accounting for 19 of 20 U.S. jobs engaged in building automobiles. And together with our dealers and suppliers, our industry employs some 2.3 million Americans.

Mr. Chairman, I want to thank you for the opportunity to testify today, but I also want to thank you for your continued leadership in bringing automotive trade with Japan to the forefront of the public agenda.

Having just returned from Tokyo this weekend, I can assure you that the public's interest in the status of the Framework negotiations in Japan is far greater than the interest that we have seen here.

As you know, within the current bilateral Framework negotiations, which are addressing the overall U.S.-Japan trade deficit, there is a separate and distinct negotiation concerning the extraordinary trade imbalance between the U.S. and Japan in automobiles and auto parts. While American car manufacturers are deeply involved and supportive of the negotiations relating to auto parts, I will focus today on trade in autos and trucks, because over $20 billion of the $34 billion bilateral automotive trade deficit is caused by the outlandish one-way trade in automobiles.

Mr. Chairman, I am here on behalf of America's car companies to deliver a simple, 4-point message. First, America's automakers are back and ready to meet any competition in the world, in every major market. Our products continue to face systemic exclusionary barriers that bar access to the Japanese market. The resulting automotive trade imbalance with Japan, which accounts for one-quarter of the entire U.S. trade deficit with the world, is unacceptable, and it must be immediately and aggressively addressed by our two Governments. And finally, all previous talks with Japan to reduce the auto trade deficit over the past decade have failed to produce results. The administration must continue to insist upon a Framework Agreement that provides clear benchmarks for measuring increased access to the Japanese automobile and auto parts market and a reduction in the trade deficit.

As a committed free-trader, I personally reject the notion that the administration's call for measuring results in improved market access is "managed trade." In fact, the most glaring example of successful managed trade in the world today is the Japanese automotive market itself, where imports from all countries—Europe, Asia and North America—total only 3 percent of the market. For instance, one country, Korea, annually exports only 300 vehicles to Japan.

What the United States seeks in these negotiations is that the Japanese Government demonstrate the same commitment and enthusiasm to creating and sustaining the conditions of a free and open market in Japan that the Japanese so vigorously pursue in the U.S. and other major markets.

Japan's Government is a strong believer in free trade in every market but its own, and we must stand firm in our commitment to bring the fruits of free trade to the Japanese consumer.

This is truly an exciting time for America's car companies. The American auto industry staged perhaps the most dramatic turnaround of any major manufacturing industry in our history, and I am proud to say that our industry did it the old-fashioned way—we met our competition head-on, listened to consumers, and regained the cutting edge in innovation and quality.

As Time Magazine recently proclaimed in a cover story, America's car companies are "on a roll." However, our success in the world's largest car market—the U.S.—and other major markets around the globe is not duplicated in the world's second-largest car market—Japan.

While Japanese carmakers have had virtually unrestricted access to the U.S. market, Japan's market is all but closed to our products. I went to Japan last week to deliver a simple message—that the Japanese consumer deserves the same chance and will benefit if given the same opportunity as consumers in other Nations to choose from the widest variety of products, including American-made cars and trucks.

And make no mistake—the Japanese consumer does not have that opportunity today. One problem that has stalled past automotive trade talks between the U.S. and Japan has been the lack of a consensus on the basic issues. It has been difficult for our two governments to agree on solutions when they could not even define the nature of the problem.

The so-called MOSS Motor Vehicle Study, commissioned jointly by both governments and paid for by the taxpayers in both countries—and I hope soon to be released—should finally put some of these extremely time-consuming debates about the nature of the problems in Japan behind us. The market is closed.

The study confirms everything that we have been saying all along, that many factors prevent Japanese consumers from having ready and open access to imported vehicles. Those factors include an exclusive locked dealership distribution system, policed by major financial ties between Japanese manufacturers and dealers. Moreover, the MOSS Study describes a Japanese buying public that is showing significant and growing interest in purchasing American and other imported cars.

This is very important. The Japanese consumer should not be forgotten in this debate.

Now, American car companies believe that if these negotiations result in serious and meaningful market-opening measures in Japan, that they can anticipate increased sales in Japan from a current annual base of between 15,000 and 20,000 units to more than 100,000 units within 3 years. The Japanese are calling this "managed trade." In fact, it is simply consumer opportunity.

American carmakers sell about 100,000 cars in Indiana each year. The question is why the Japanese are absolutely stonewalling such a modest goal when they have a 6 million unit car market.

We are asking not for guaranteed sales, but for equal opportunity. We believe our products will sell themselves if given that opportunity.

So there is no question that American automakers are interested and committed to selling in the Japanese market; we are. The globally-competitive economics of the auto industry, and the importance of the Asia-Pacific Region as a future growth market alone require these commitments.

The real question is how will Japan respond. The question still remains very much unanswered, and that is why AAMA, along with its member companies—Chrysler, Ford and GM—believe that the only agreement worth signing is one which establishes clear and meaningful targets to measure Japan's success in opening its market to imported vehicles and parts.

Now, the President and the Prime Minister incorporated this objective by calling for "the establishment of objective criteria, either qualitative or quantitative, or both, to be used for the purpose of evaluating progress in each sectoral and structural area." That is a quote from a joint statement by the President and the Prime Minister.

We support the three fundamental goals as outlined originally by the U.S. negotiators—increased sales of American vehicles in Japan; increased sales of American parts in Japan, and increased sales of American parts to transplants located in the United States. These were the administration's original goals, and we continue to support them. And if they are not achieved, we will applaud a decision to walk away from the bargaining table.

Finally, let me emphasize that neither we nor our Government is suggesting that Japanese consumers somehow should be pressured or forced to buy American products. We simply seek the credible opportunity to reach Japanese consumers, discuss with them their questions and their needs, and show them what American consumers and American workers have together created—a wide range of quality products, aimed at meeting a variety of car buyers' needs.

Japanese consumers are like American consumers. They want good value at a good price. We can deliver that value, but the current barriers deny us an opportunity to deliver them at a competitive price.

While in Tokyo, I had the pleasure of addressing a group of students at Keio University. They had read about our cars, but had never had the opportunity to experience them in the dealer's showroom or in the marketplace. And like one of the students said to me: "Okyaku-sama wa kamisama desu."

The translation: "The customer is God."

We agree. The Japanese customer deserves the same chance to purchase American-made cars that American consumers have to purchase Japanese-made cars. An opportunity like that can only be met with successful Framework negotiations. We need it, and the Japanese consumer deserves to have it, but the American worker will benefit most from it.

Thank you, Mr. Chairman. I look forward to responding to your questions.

Senator LEVIN. Thank you, Mr. Card. I have just a couple questions, because we have a vote now in the Senate, but I do want to have you do two things for me. One is—although I am familiar with it, but for the record—outline some of the barriers that exist

76-349 O - 95 - 2

to our automobiles being made available to the consumer in Japan; and second, whether or not you agree that the only way we are going to get a successful negotiation is if we inform the Japanese what will happen in the event we are not going to get a successful negotiation.

Mr. CARD. First with regard to the barriers, logic tells you there is a barrier when we are able to service only .5 percent of a 6 million-unit car market when in every other industrial market in the world, imports make up between 20 and 55 percent of the marketplace. All imports into Japan represent only 3 percent of the market.

Some of the barriers that exist are barriers of practice, and we found an awful lot of experience where dealers do not believe that they have the right to even negotiate with importers to sell imported vehicles in Japan; a practical barrier of access to the consumer. The MOSS Study, again, reflects some of those problems.

There are barriers that relate to how a vehicle is allowed to come into the marketplace, the certification process. Japanese vehicles that come into the United States are self-certified; they go right from the ship to the showroom in the United States. An American-made vehicle does not go from the ship to the showroom in Japan. In some cases, there are individual vehicle certifications that are necessary; in only a few instances, there have been some "type" certifications—but even these did not foster a quick, easy access to the marketplace.

We also know there are dealer-manufacturer arrangements in Japan that are very much unlike dealer-manufacturer relationships in the United States. In Japan, 25 percent of the dealers are owned 100 percent by the manufacturers. Many of the other dealers have financial arrangements with manufacturers that are in the 40 to 60 percent range.

Therefore, there is a belief among many dealers that there would be some economic problem if they were to allow imported vehicles to be shown in their showroom or distributed through their fliers.

Those are practical concerns. The markup on vehicles going into the Japanese market today, based on the barriers that exist, represents between 26 and 42 percent of the cost of the vehicle. That is a huge burden for the consumer to carry. That burden——

Senator LEVIN. And it also keeps down your car sales.

Mr. CARD. It reduces our car sales, and we do not have the access to the consumer the way Japanese manufacturers have access to our consumers.

With regard to what should come next if these trade talks are not successful, the status quo is unacceptable. The status quo defines the problem. So I would hope that our Government would take a serious look at the problem and see if there are other ways to generate a solution.

There are two ways to measure success—market sales and trade deficit reductions. Those are the only two viable measurements of success. What is happening in the marketplace? Are American-made cars available to the consumers so that they can exercise their choice to buy them? And is the trade deficit being reduced?

Those are the only two measurements that have credibility, and I have been around a long time, as you have, Mr. Chairman, watching these trade talks. We have heard a lot of rhetoric; we have not seen any performance. The problem today is no more solved than the problem was years and years ago.

Senator LEVIN. Well, I agree that if we do not get a good result, we ought to walk away. I also happen to feel very strongly that we will not get a good result unless we let them know, going in, what will happen if there is no negotiated agreement. Otherwise, we are just not even telling them critical information to them in making up their own mind.

Mr. Card, thank you. Five bells have run, and as you well know from your past experience in Washington, that means we have got to get our roller skates on.

Thank you for coming.

Mr. CARD. Thank you, Senator.

Senator LEVIN. We stand adjourned.

[Whereupon, at 11:32 a.m., the Subcommittee was adjourned.]

APPENDIX

WRITTEN TESTIMONY OF THE HONORABLE

JEFFREY E. GARTEN

UNDER SECRETARY FOR INTERNATIONAL TRADE

U.S. DEPARTMENT OF COMMERCE

BEFORE THE

SENATE SUBCOMMITTEE

ON OVERSIGHT OF GOVERNMENT MANAGEMENT

February 3, 1994

I appreciate the opportunity to testify before this subcommittee on the Administration's efforts to deal with the long-standing bilateral automotive trade problems with Japan. At the outset, I would like to acknowledge that members of this committee are no strangers to these issues. I know that my predecessors have worked closely with you and many of your colleagues since automotive negotiations with Japan began in 1986.

The intense interest shown by you, Mr. Chairman, your subcommittee, and the Congress in general has provided the consistency of message and intensity of purpose necessary to communicate to the Japanese that we are serious about resolving these matters. We need your continued interest and support if there is to be a successful agreement.

You can also take credit for the excellent advice and assistance provided by our industry over the years through the Auto Parts Advisory Committee. It was the Fair Trade in Auto Parts Act of 1988 that made this valuable resource available to U.S. Government negotiators. Let me say here, that whether or not we conclude a Framework Agreement with the Japanese next week, I would like to continue to count on the Auto Parts Advisory Committee for advice. Since the authority for that advisory group expired at the end of last year, I am hoping for quick action by the Congress to reauthorize it for another five years. Mr. Chairman, I appreciate your introduction of legislation last week to re-authorize the Committee.

BACKGROUND ON U.S.-JAPAN AUTO TRADE

Since 1986, the automotive trade imbalance has accounted for at least 40 percent of our global merchandise trade deficit. This includes all motor vehicles and automotive parts. The automotive portion of the deficit peaked at 67 percent in 1991, and fell to 43 percent in 1993, in large part because the non-automotive deficit increased (See chart).

Most of the U.S. automotive trade deficit since the early 1980's has been with Japan:

* In 1990, the automotive sector accounted for 75 percent of the total U.S.-Japan merchandise trade deficit; in 1993, it was 62 percent; (See chart).

* Based on value, the automotive deficit with Japan has increased from $30.8 billion in 1990 to an estimated $33.5 billion for 1993, and is expected to deteriorate further in 1994 to over $35 billion.

* For motor vehicles, the estimated trade imbalance will exceed $24 billion in 1994. Although the actual number of vehicles imported from Japan has steadily declined, the value of these vehicles has increased -- from $22.2 billion in 1990 to an estimated $24.5 billion in 1994 -

- due to a shift in product mix to more expensive models.

* Even more disturbing is the trend in parts, where the trade imbalance is projected to increase from $9.5 billion in 1990 to an estimated $12.2 billion in 1994.

Although the Japanese vehicle manufacturers have increased their purchases of U.S. parts from $1.7 billion in 1985 to an estimated $14.5 billion in 1993 (based on Japanese Automobile Manufacturers Association data), this increase has done little to lower the U.S.-Japan automotive parts trade deficit. Production at the Japanese transplants has increased much more rapidly than transplant U.S. parts content, resulting in an expanding deficit.

The problem has been persistent and indeed has grown since the late 1970's, despite various efforts by government to address it. For example:

* Government-to-government discussions have been conducted under the Market-Oriented Sector-Selective Talks on Transportation Machinery and ensuing follow-up talks since 1986.

* The Market-Oriented Cooperation Plan was negotiated in 1990 to consolidate ongoing and newly suggested programs into a plan of action. As part of this Plan, the Government of Japan agreed to provide to the U.S. Government the Japanese auto makers' plans for U.S. procurement and to undertake a joint study of factors affecting the sale of foreign vehicles in Japan.

* A joint Department of Commerce and Ministry of International Trade and Industry price survey of four auto parts was conducted in 1991. The prices of surveyed auto parts in Japan were on average 340 percent higher than in the United States, demonstrating the Japanese consumer has been paying a heavy price because of the closed Japanese market.

* The Department of Commerce and Ministry of International Trade and Industry sponsored auto parts conferences on how to do business with the Japanese vehicle manufacturers. All four were well attended, with the most recent held last year in Dearborn, Michigan, attracting over 500 attendees. A fifth conference is tentatively scheduled for October of this year, also to be held in Dearborn.

* During a Presidential visit to Japan in January, 1992, the Government of Japan announced the Global Partnership Plan of Action. As part of this Plan, Japanese vehicle manufacturers stated that they would voluntarily increase their purchases of U.S. parts from an estimated $9 billion in 1990 to $19 billion in 1994. The Plan also stated that the Japanese vehicle producers in the United States plan to increase their U.S. content from 50 percent in 1990 to 70 percent by 1994.

Yet despite all these efforts, the automotive trade deficit continues at an exceptionally high level, and we have not achieved significantly improved market access into the Japanese automotive market.

THE FRAMEWORK NEGOTIATIONS

Last July, President Clinton and Japanese Prime Minister Miyazawa announced the U.S.-Japan Framework for a New Economic Partnership. The Framework is intended to address critical economic issues with the overall goal of strengthening the bilateral economic relationship and enhancing the world trading system. A primary objective of the Framework negotiations is to remove structural barriers that prevent expanded trade and investment flows in key industries such as autos. Automotive issues were selected as "high-priority," and an agreement is scheduled to be concluded by February 11--the next meeting of the President and Japanese Prime Minister.

To date, it seems that the Government of Japan is still seeking to re-negotiate the terms of the original Framework document. It has repeatedly stated that their role as a government is limited, and that we should negotiate removal of trade barriers to our market as well.

The Framework calls on the U.S. to reduce its fiscal deficit over the medium term. We are, as you know, making meaningful progress. The Clinton Administration's economic plan will reduce the deficit by $500 billion over five years. The 1995 fiscal year deficit is now projected to be less than $180 billion, down from a projected $300 billion before the President's plan was adopted last year. That's a reduction of 40 percent. If we continue with this plan, the deficit will be cut in half as a percentage of U.S. national income by 1996.

The Framework calls on the U.S. to "strengthen its international competitiveness." The deficit reduction, the emphasis on education and training, the focus on technology policies all help to achieve this goal. In addition, the Administration has placed a high priority on improving U.S. Government export promotion programs. These programs must be designed to ensure that U.S. products and services reach markets around the world, thereby creating jobs at home. The Trade Promotion Coordinating Committee is chaired by Secretary Brown and is composed of 19 U.S. Government Agencies involved in trade promotion. Last September, it issued a report, "Toward a National Export Strategy," which contained 65 specific recommendations to rationalize and strengthen U.S. Government promotion efforts. We are in the process of vigorously implementing these recommendations.

As part of that export strategy, we have developed a variety of programs to promote and support the sale of U.S. products in the Japanese market. Our Foreign Commercial Service presence in Japan is the largest in any country. In addition, the Department of Commerce maintains several programs specifically aimed at Japan -- including the Japan Export Promotion Program and the Japan Corporate Program.

Our promotion programs for Japan will benefit from the rationalization and improvement measures contained in the Trade Policy Coordinating Committee's recommendations. We are currently discussing these programs and other promotional and competitiveness enhancement efforts relating to Japan in the Framework negotiations. Effective export promotion programs to follow up on Framework agreements will be important to ensure real results for our firms.

THE U.S. AUTOMOTIVE PROPOSAL

To address market access problems in the automotive sector we have presented the Japanese with a comprehensive proposal that focuses on three areas: auto parts sales, vehicle sales, and deregulation. I should point out that it is the stated objective of Japanese industry and government to increase "localization" of overseas production and to deregulate their economy. I believe the U.S. proposal is consistent with these Japanese objectives and can in fact accelerate achievement of their goals.

There are four critical components to the U.S. proposal:

1) Providing access to the Japanese vehicle distribution system through a significant increase in the number of direct franchise agreements between Japanese dealers and foreign vehicle manufacturers;

2) Continuing and improving on the trend of increasing North American content by Japanese manufacturers located in the United States;

3) Continuing and improving on the trend of increasing purchases of U.S. manufactured auto parts by Japanese vehicle manufacturers located in Japan and the United States; and,

4) Achieving significant regulatory reform, deregulation, and simplification of Japanese Government procedures in the areas of standards, certification, and the parts aftermarket.

In addition to these four critical elements, the U.S. proposal also calls for:

* Opening Japanese procurement and design-in processes to foreign auto parts suppliers by providing information about upcoming procurements;

* Expanding Japanese engineering and technical exchanges with U.S. parts suppliers;

* Continuing the trend of increasing U.S. exports from Japanese vehicle manufacturers located in the United States;

* expanding business relationships between U.S. and Japanese automotive companies in Japan and throughout East Asia; and,

* stronger enforcement of Japan's antitrust laws with respect to the Japanese automotive industry.

Consistent with the overall Framework Agreement, the U.S. proposal contains multiple quantitative and qualitative criteria for assessing progress in as many of these areas as possible. We believe it is important that we are able to monitor progress and have the capacity to determine whether the goals of this arrangement are achieved. These actions and others suggested by the United States are intended to achieve the objective of "unmanaging" trade by increasing market access and sales opportunities in Japan for foreign automotive products in manner consistent with our obligations in GATT and elsewhere. In order for the automotive discussions to be a success, at a minimum we require a standard for the tangible progress that must be achieved and a timeframe for achieving that standard. I have explained this to the Japanese on several occasions.

THE JAPANESE AUTOMOTIVE PROPOSAL

In contrast to the U.S. proposal, Japan's counterproposal has emphasized analysis of historic data rather than achieving progress which can be judged against objective criteria. The Japanese government has insisted upon an approach which would make the examination of U.S. sales efforts a focal point of any agreement. They have resisted, point by point, our proposals to eliminate Japan's market access barriers. In general, the Japanese negotiators hold to the view that there are no barriers, only a lack of understanding on the part of the U.S. Government and industry about Japanese companies and the Japanese market, or a lack of effort on the part of U.S. companies to enter the Japanese market. The Japanese proposal fails to acknowledge or address the fundamental impediments limiting equal access to the Japanese market and contains no objective criteria by which future progress can be measured.

THE EFFORTS OF U.S. INDUSTRY

Private sector efforts have been, and will continue to be, crucial to the ultimate success and effectiveness of any Framework Agreement. It is clear to me that U.S. companies are making strong efforts to obtain business in Japan. For example:

* Chrysler introduced a right hand drive Cherokee a year ago in Japan and sales growth has been impressive. Chrysler will begin selling right hand drive versions of the Grand Cherokee and Jeep Wrangler in 1994.

* This year Ford will begin exporting from the United States right hand drive version of the Probe. Within three years, Ford will be building, in the United States, right hand drive Tauruses and Explorers for export to Japan.

* Last July, Ford announced plans to build a $50 million technical center near Tokyo. This year, Ford Motor Credit Corporation will begin operations in Japan; the company will extend financing to dealers and customers in Japan.

* General Motors has announced plans to export right hand drive Chevy Cavaliers to Japan beginning in 1996. These cars will be sold under the Toyota nameplate.

These efforts are particularly impressive when one takes into account the large capital expenditures required and the fact that the Detroit-based manufacturers currently account for only 0.3 percent of the Japanese market.

Japanese officials have themselves acknowledged the closing of the quality gap between Japanese produced and U.S. produced vehicles. There is a great deal of independent analysis to support this view. The buying public's assessment of the quality of Big-Three brands, as measured by J.D. Power and Associates' New Car Customer Satisfaction Index, has risen from a level of 94 in 1986 to 132 in 1993. This represents an improvement of 40 percent. The Index for Japanese-brands increased just 18 percent during the same period. While the Japanese Index remains marginally higher, many consumers consider the differences to be insignificant given the price advantages of Big-Three vehicles. Perhaps most telling is the fact that Detroit-based manufacturers are recapturing market share (four percentage points in the last two years) from Japanese manufacturers in the United States.

CONSULTATION EFFORTS

The Department of Commerce has consulted closely with both U.S. and Japanese private sectors throughout these negotiations and meetings have picked up in frequency as the Framework process has progressed. In addition, we have encouraged and received broad interagency participation on this issue from the beginning.

Since my confirmation by the Senate in November, I have met personally with as many representatives of U.S. industry as I could. Regarding auto parts, I have met with the Auto Parts Advisory Committee, representatives of the major parts trade associations, the UAW, and individual company executives. Just last week I talked with a group of seven business leaders in the parts industry. Concerning vehicles, I have traveled to Detroit to consult with senior officials from General Motors, Ford and Chrysler and have met on a number of occasions in Washington with their trade association, the American Automobile Manufacturers Association. Last week I met with a bipartisan group of Representatives and Senators, including the Chairman of this subcommittee, which was organized by Northeast-Midwest Congressional Coalition.

In addition, I have met extensively with the senior management of Japanese companies and their vehicle and parts trade associations both here and in Japan. On my first trip to Japan in December, I met with the Executive Committee of the Japan Automobile Manufacturers Association and the Japan Automotive Parts Industry Association. I also held private meetings with the leaders of the major individual Japanese auto companies. These meetings continued on my second visit in January. This week I have been holding individual meetings with the senior management of their U.S. subsidiaries.

The purpose of these meetings is to explain the U.S. position directly to the Japanese companies that will be implementing many of our specific proposals. Their cooperation is necessary to open the vehicle and the parts markets in Japan, as well as at the U.S. transplants. My message has been that the U.S. proposal reflects necessary structural changes and that the current recession in Japan ought not be an excuse for further delay.

While our primary objective in these negotiations is to open the Japanese market to create opportunities for increased sales of U.S. parts and vehicles, we believe that our proposal will benefit both the U.S. and Japanese industries. We believe that the U.S. proposal will result in expanded U.S. sales and U.S. exports which in turn will mean increased jobs and profits in the United States. We also believe that the market opening and deregulatory measures we are seeking will lower costs to Japanese manufacturers and result in substantial benefits to Japanese consumers. Furthermore, both industries will benefit from increased cooperation and interaction, which is already a significant trend in the global auto industry. This is the message I have attempted to convey in my many meetings with Japanese government officials and industry representatives.

CURRENT STATUS

I cannot say to you today that we are close to an agreement. Despite the intensive discussions and negotiations held almost continuously since July, not to mention the years of previous discussion, we do not seem to have even a common understanding of the problem, let alone consensus on the solutions.

At the moment, there is a huge gap between our positions. Concluding a meaningful agreement by next week's summit meeting between President Clinton and Prime Minister Hosokawa will be extremely difficult. We believe that it is better to have no agreement at this time than to have one that fails to address the underlying problems, or one that provides no way to measure progress. The long history of this issue is filled with agreements that have, at best, only partially removed the fundamental barriers to free trade in the automotive sector. If we find that no agreement is possible at this time, we will of course want to consider our alternatives and to consult with the Congress about how to proceed. We remain determined to continue to work toward an agreement that will give competitive U.S. vehicle and parts manufacturers the same access in Japan that Japanese manufacturers have enjoyed in the U.S. market.

Thank you and I look forward to your questions.

Motor Vehicle and Parts Share of the U.S. Merchandise Trade Deficit

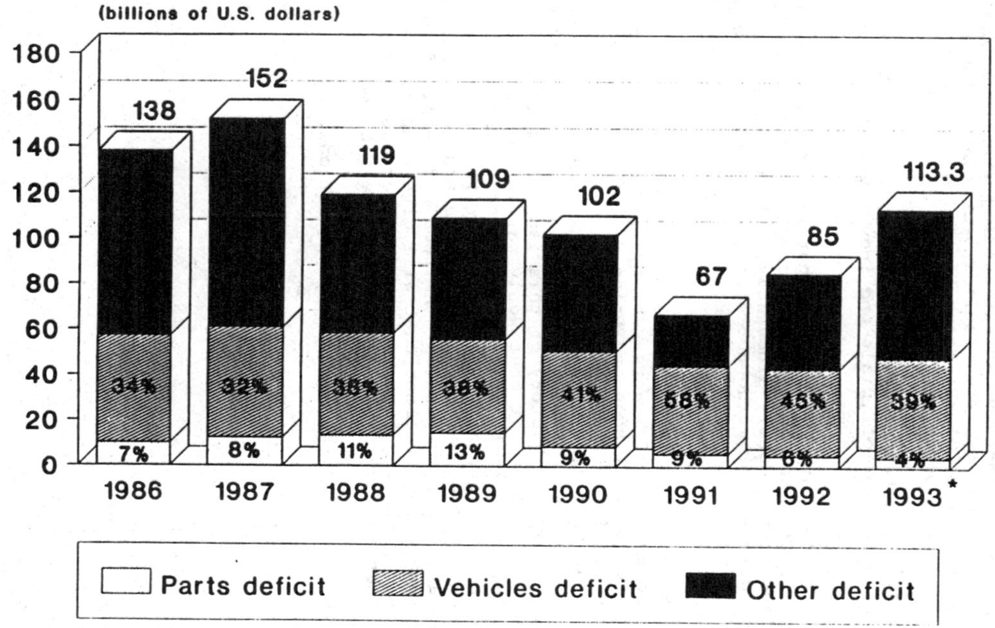

Source: U.S. Census Bureau

*Estimated from Jan.-Sept. 1993 data

Motor Vehicle and Parts Share of the U.S.-Japan Merchandise Trade Deficit

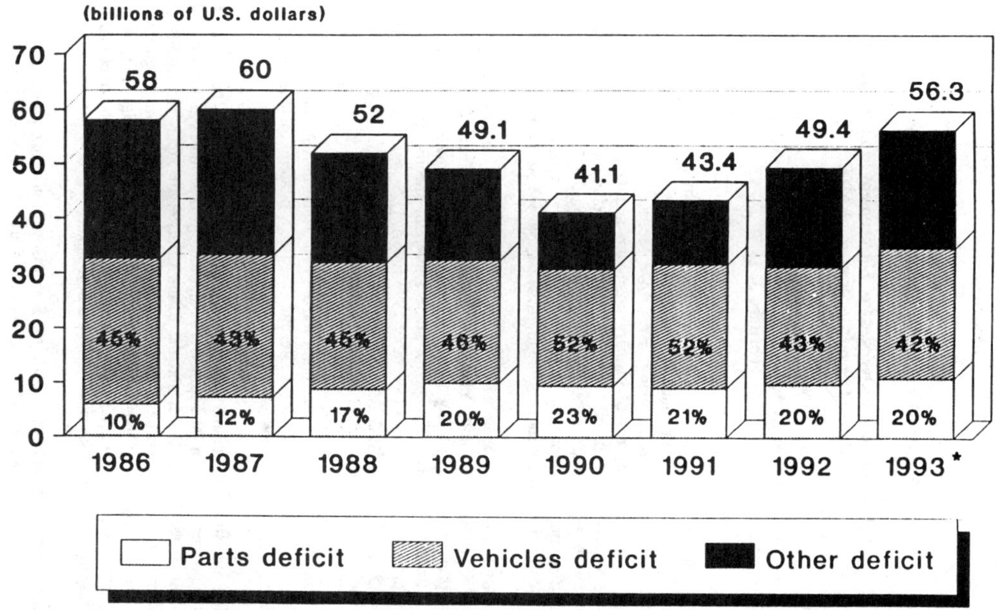

Source: U.S. Census Bureau
•Estimated from Jan.-Sept. 1993 data

Statement of
Robert E. Cole
Vice President, Government Affairs
Kaiser Aluminum & Chemical Corporation
Presented to the
Subcommittee on Oversight of Government Management
Committee on Governmental Affairs
United States Senate
Hearing on
U.S.-Japan Auto Parts Framework Negotiations
February 3, 1994

Mr. Chairman and Members of the Subcommittee, I am Robert E. Cole, Vice President for Government Affairs, Kaiser Aluminum & Chemical Corporation and Vice President for Federal Government Affairs of its parent company, MAXXAM Inc. Kaiser Aluminum is one of the world's leading, fully integrated producers of primary aluminum and fabricated aluminum products. We produce a wide variety of automobile parts and materials including forgings, extrusions, castings, sheet, rod, bar, wire, and primary metal. We supply products in the Original Equipment (OE) market directly to auto assembly companies, to first and second tier suppliers and through independent distributors. We also have some sales in the aftermarket, but we are primarily OE suppliers.

For several years I have been a member of the Auto Parts Advisory Committee (APAC), established pursuant to the Omnibus Trade and Competitiveness Act of 1988 (P.L. 100-410). I appreciate the opportunity to present testimony today on APAC's most recent report to the Secretary of Commerce on auto parts trade with Japan. Except for some aluminum specific statements, my statement is essentially a summary of the APAC's December 1993 report, U.S-Japan Auto Parts Trade Five Years After The Fair Trade In Auto Parts Act: A Results Oriented Review. The full report is also being submitted to the Subcommittee.

The year 1993 marks both the five year point for the Fair Trade in Auto Parts Act initiative and the beginning of the Clinton Administration's "Results Oriented", bilateral trade negotiations with Japan, under the United States-Japan Framework for a New Economic Partnership.

The automotive industries, including both the motor vehicle and the auto parts sectors, have been designated as major sectors under the Framework Negotiations. The joint statement issued in July 1993 by the President of the United States and the Prime Minister of Japan specifically stated that the bilateral government efforts "will have the objective, inter alia of achieving significantly expanded sales opportunities to result in a significant expansion of purchases of foreign parts by Japanese firms in Japan and through their transplants, as well as removing problems which affect market access, and encouraging imports of foreign autos and auto parts in Japan."

To help accomplish these objectives, the United States Government has presented the Japanese with a comprehensive proposal on autos and auto parts that focuses on three main areas:

Purchases of U.S. auto parts by Japanese transplant vehicle manufacturers,
Purchases of Foreign Auto Parts in Japan, and
Imports of Foreign Vehicles by Japan.

The achievement of the U.S. objectives in the Framework Negotiations is very important to the success of the Clinton Administration's programs for revitalization of the domestic economy in the United States, expanding U.S. exports, and guiding the post Cold War transition of persons employed in the military and defense industry to civilian employment. The U.S. proposal should also be compatible with the Hosokawa Administration's objectives of political and regulatory reform and transforming the export oriented Japanese economy to a more consumer oriented economy.

The motor vehicle and auto parts industries are essential to the health of the American economy. Expansion of job opportunities for American workers and expansion of business opportunities for American owners and stockholders of auto parts companies are essential to any program to grow the American economy. Preservation and strengthening of the technological capabilities existing in the American motor vehicle and auto parts industries are essential as the foundation for technology transfer to other manufacturing industries having significant growth potential for the American economy.

Manufacturing in the automotive and allied industries employs one million persons, equal to approximately seven percent of total manufacturing employment in the U.S. economy.

The U.S. auto industry provides high value-added jobs with well above average pay, health benefits, and pension benefits.

The traditional sector of the industry accounts for about eleven percent of corporate R&D and employs approximately six percent of all scientists and engineers.

Over 5,000 U.S. owned companies conduct substantial business in the industry.

The auto parts sector is a diverse $100 billion industry.

No other economic sectors in the United States have anywhere near the potential of the motor vehicle and auto parts industries to grow through increased exports and displacement of imports to accomplish the domestic economic recovery and defense conversion goals of the Clinton Administration and the Congress.

Exports of U.S. auto parts have grown substantially since 1988, accounting for approximately $33.1 billion in U.S. exports in 1993.

Since 1989, the United States would have run an overall trade surplus in auto parts each year, except for the large trade deficit with Japan. The deficit with Japan was $11 billion in 1993, compared with $8.8 billion in 1988. Studies for APAC by the Office for the Study of Automotive Transportation of the University of Michigan Transportation Research Institute project that the auto parts deficit with Japan will likely remain at current very high levels or worsen during the next several years.

The trade deficits with Japan and accompanying economic dislocations in the United States are persistent despite dramatic and well documented improvements in the competitiveness of the American auto parts industry, especially in the areas which the Japanese vehicle manufacturers have traditionally stated were the critical factors in selection of suppliers -price, quality, and deliverability--and despite American industry leadership in the newest high technology areas such as airbags, antilock braking systems, and lightweight materials. The trade deficit is growing despite dramatic changes in the Yen-Dollar ratios in recent years, which have favored U.S. manufactured products.

In the five years since the enactment of the Fair Trade in Auto Parts Act, the American government and industry have conducted numerous studies of the competitiveness of the U.S. auto parts industry and of the barriers to trade with the Japanese in both the original equipment markets and the aftermarkets in the U.S. and in Japan. The problems confronted by traditional U.S. manufacturers are numerous and well documented. (A list of major studies is presented in the Bibliography section of the 1993 APAC Report)

U.S. auto parts manufacturers and their employees have experienced serious economic dislocation due to the lack of meaningful access to the Japanese market and to structural barriers (such as the exclusionary practices of Japanese "keiretsu" groups linking vehicle and parts manufacturers in Japan and the United States) which limit access to Japanese subsidiaries and affiliates in North America and key emerging automotive markets in developing countries.

Since 1988, the United States and Japanese Governments also have conducted a variety of bilateral trade negotiations which have sought to increase trade and identify and rectify both generic trade barriers and auto sector specific trade barriers, including:

Market-Oriented Sector Selective Transportation
Machinery Talks (MOSS)
Market-Oriented Cooperation Plan (MOCP)
Structural Impediments Initiative (SII)
Auto Parts Sector Negotiations under the
Framework Agreement

The last five years of negotiations are not the first wave of bilateral, U.S.-Japan negotiations on auto parts. The first negotiations were the 1981-1983 U.S.-Japan Trade Facilitation Committee Negotiations on Auto Parts, which were actually terminated in 1981 at Japan's insistence.

A significant advance in the efforts to increase trade in auto parts occurred in January of 1992 when Prime Minister Miyazawa and President Bush announced their nations' commitments to the Global Partnership and the Global Partnership Plan of Action. That Plan of Action included descriptions of the Japanese car companies' "voluntary purchase plans" for buying $19 billion in U.S. auto parts, in 1994.

The government and industry efforts which culminated in the Japanese-U.S. Action Plan's JFY 1994 parts purchase goals set the stage for substantial progress to be made in the current U.S.-Japan Framework Negotiations if both the U.S. and Japanese Governments are truly committed and remain persistent in their efforts to resolve trade issues and remove trade barriers.

Major improvements in U.S.-Japan auto parts trade remain to be accomplished. Even if the 1994 voluntary plans are met by the Japanese vehicle manufacturers, which remains in doubt, the Japanese transplant vehicle manufacturing operations in the United States are projected to utilize imported parts for 30 percent of total parts purchases. Total auto parts imports from Japan are estimated to have been $12.1 billion in 1993. The JAMA 1994 voluntary plans did not break out purchases from traditional vs. transplant suppliers in the U.S. However, according to a JAMA report, traditional U.S. suppliers currently supply an estimated 26 percent of the transplants' parts purchases, with over half of the Japanese transplant vehicle manufacturers' U.S. parts purchases coming from the increasing number of Japanese transplant parts suppliers. In Japan, imported parts still account for less than two percent of the over $160 billion auto parts and accessories market.

Two years have passed since the Japanese government and vehicle manufacturers announced their voluntary plans for JFY 1994. No such announcements have been made for JFY 1995 or JFY 1996. Nor have other significant achievements been made in bilateral auto parts negotiations with Japan in the past two years.

The United States cannot afford to repeat the mistake of the early 1980's, when bilateral trade negotiations with Japan on auto parts were abandoned.

Regrettably, to date the Japanese Government's and the Japan Automobile Manufacturers Association's responses to the U.S. Government's auto and auto parts sector proposals under the Framework Negotiations have been very disappointing.

The opportunities that currently exist for growth in employment, ownership and technological capabilities in the U.S. motor vehicle and auto parts industries and the associated benefits to the United States economy and the American public need to be achieved. But those benefits can be achieved only if the United States and Japanese governments implement policies to effectively and expeditiously remove the already well documented barriers to increased exports of American made auto parts to Japan and to increased sales of American made auto parts to the Japanese transplant motor vehicle industry in the U.S.

Kaiser Aluminum is one of several U.S. aluminum companies that are implementing comprehensive programs to substantially expand business with the Japanese vehicle industry. Kaiser has an office in Tokyo, Japan. Kaiser has formed a Tokyo based joint venture company, called the Furukawa Kaiser Forged Products Company, with the Furukawa Electric Co., Ltd., and the Itochu Corporation to serve the Japanese ground transportation industry and other selected Asian markets. Kaiser also has an agreement with Furukawa Electric Co. Ltd., Kawasaki Steel Corporation, and Pechiney Rhenalu (a member of France's Pechiney Group) to develop aluminum automotive body sheet superior to products currently available and to make the cost of aluminum body panels more competitive. Several Kaiser business units are working directly with Japanese vehicle manufacturers including Toyota, Mazda, and Honda on possible business. Kaiser has had extensive and cordial business discussions with the Japanese companies and some of our facilities and products have been extensively evaluated.

Unfortunately, Kaiser's activities have not yet resulted in any firm business for either Kaiser directly or our Tokyo based joint venture company. However, we remain committed to the business efforts. We know we are competitive, and we are determined to be successful.

Like others in the U.S. auto parts industry, we at Kaiser are anxiously watching the Framework Negotiations and sincerely hoping they will be successful.

The Auto Parts Advisory Committee has made extensive and cohesive Policy Recommendations to the Secretary of Commerce for actions to increase trade with Japan in the U.S. and in the Japanese domestic market. The Policy Recommendations have been reviewed and updated during 1993 and are applicable to the current Framework Negotiations. APAC's policies reflect strong support for open markets for motor vehicles and auto parts, in which success is achievable through fair and open competition among manufacturers. APAC members are confident that the U.S. auto parts industry can successfully compete in every automotive market in the world if competition is not restricted by non-market barriers or exclusionary practices either imposed or tolerated by national governments. APAC strongly recommends that prompt removal of such barriers and exclusionary practices must be a major objective of the U.S. government.

APAC has strongly recommended that the U.S. Government:

(1) Continue to insist on achievement of the Japanese U.S. parts purchasing and local content targets with special emphasis on traditional U.S. suppliers set for fiscal year 1994;

(2) Take other interim steps -including opening the original equipment and aftermarket in Japan to U.S. suppliers and continuous improvements in expanded purchases and design-in relationships with U.S. suppliers in North America- necessary to reach an equitable and sustainable auto parts trade relationship with Japan by 1998;

(3) These actions should facilitate agreement with the Japanese Government, in cooperation with U.S. and Japanese industry, to achieve major annual reductions in the massive and growing U.S. auto parts trade deficit with Japan over a five-year period to a level which reflects U.S. industry's strong international competitive position and is consistent with other major U.S. bilateral trading relationships; and

(4) Monitor, in cooperation with U.S. industry on a regular basis, the progress which non-Japanese affiliated U.S. automotive suppliers are making in expanding original equipment and aftermarket sales and business relationships with Japanese companies in the United States and Japan.

APAC has supported a Clinton Administration review of the options for U.S. actions (including U.S. government self-initiation of trade actions such as anti-dumping, section 301, and proposed Super 301 extension) against any country, including Japan, which does not live up to its fair trade obligations as a major participant in the global auto parts market.

APAC also supports extension of the Fair Trade in Auto Parts Act, which was requested of Congress by the Clinton Administration in October, 1993. The U.S. Government's trade efforts must be persistent and the close industry-government cooperation (which has been exceptionally strong since the establishment of APAC) must continue if the U.S. government and U.S. auto parts industry are to achieve their mutual objectives for economic growth, high-quality employment, competition-based business opportunities and leading-edge technological advances that historically have provided enormous benefits to the American people in our consumer-oriented economy.

U.S.-JAPAN AUTO PARTS TRADE

FIVE YEARS AFTER

THE FAIR TRADE IN AUTO PARTS ACT

A Results Oriented Review

By the Auto Parts Advisory Committee

1993 ANNUAL REPORT OF
THE AUTO PARTS ADVISORY COMMITTEE
TO THE SECRETARY OF COMMERCE
DECEMBER 1993

APAC
Auto
Parts
Advisory
Committee

December 27, 1993

The Honorable Ronald H. Brown
Secretary of Commerce
14th Street and Constitution Avenue, N.W.
Room 5858
Washington, DC 20230

Dear Secretary Brown:

Enclosed is the document, "U.S.-Japan Auto Parts Trade, Five Years After the Fair Trade in Auto Parts Act: A Results Oriented Review by the Auto Parts Advisory Committee." This is the 1993 APAC Report to the Secretary of Commerce, submitted pursuant to sections 2123 and 2124 of the Omnibus Trade and Competitiveness Act of 1988 (P.L. 100-410).

The Auto Parts Advisory Committee is pleased to have prepared this Annual Report to assist the Commerce Department in reporting to the Congress on the progress of U.S.-made auto parts sales to Japanese markets worldwide and the state of the U.S. auto parts industry. I commend the report to the Department's attention and respectfully request that it be forwarded to the Congress.

The year 1993 marks the five-year point of the Congressionally mandated FTAPA initiative and the beginning of the Clinton Administration's "Results Oriented" bilateral trade negotiations with Japan, under the United States-Japan Framework for a New Economic Partnership. The members of the APAC strongly support the "Results Oriented" approach of the U.S. Government and are very pleased that the automotive and auto parts industries have been selected as major sectors for priority attention in the Framework Negotiations. We believe the government and industry efforts during the last five years have set the stage for substantial progress to be made in the current U.S.-Japan Framework Negotiations.

APAC also supports extension of the Fair Trade in Auto Parts Act until December 31, 1998, which was requested of Congress by the Clinton Administration in October 1993.

On behalf of APAC, I want to thank you for the attention and assistance which the Department of Commerce has given to the APAC and to the extremely important issue of increasing opportunities for U.S. auto parts sales to the Japanese.

Sincerely,

J.P. Reilly
Chairman
Auto Parts Advisory Committee

JPR/mbm

Enclosure

PREFACE

The Auto Parts Advisory Committee (APAC) is pleased to have prepared this 1993 Annual Report to assist the Secretary of Commerce in reporting to Congress on the progress of U.S.-made auto parts sales to Japanese markets and the state of the U.S. automotive supplier industry. This report is submitted pursuant to Sections 2123 and 2124 of the Omnibus Trade and Competitiveness Act of 1988 (P.L. 100-410).

The Auto Parts Advisory Committee (APAC) is a national advisory committee established by the Fair Trade in Auto Parts Act included in the Omnibus Trade and Competitiveness Act of 1988 (P.L. 100-410). The Committee advises the Department of Commerce on programs to increase sales of U.S.-made auto parts and accessories to Japanese automotive manufacturers world wide. APAC members are private sector representatives who receive no government compensation for their membership on the Committee. The views expressed in this report do not necessarily reflect those of the Administration or individual members of the Auto Parts Advisory Committee.

John P. Reilly, APAC Chairman
Robert E. Cole, Annual Report Task Force Chairman
Lee Kadrich, Task Force Vice Chairman
Steven M. Beckman, Task Force Member
J. Bernard Reilly, Task Force Member
Christopher M. Bates, Advisor

AUTO PARTS ADVISORY COMMITTEE
MEMBERSHIP LIST
(Membership terms expire on December 31, 1993)

Member's Name	Organization
Beckman, Steven M.	United Auto Workers
Bowden, Bruce K.	Stant Manufacturing, Inc.
Brewer, Thomas	Georgetown University
Burns, Jack	Security Chain Company
Cole, Robert E.	Kaiser Aluminum & Chemical Corporation
Cowie, Robert A.	Consultant
Cutler, Ronald L.	TRW Automotive Sector
Diaz, Alvaro A.	Silberline Manufacturing Co., Inc.
Fricke, Philip K.	Prudential-Bache Securities Research
Goode, Dr. John M.	Consultant
Grant, Mark	National Semiconductor
Gualdoni, Robert L.	Compass Group Ltd.
Kadrich, Lee	Auto Parts & Accessories Association
Malus, Joseph	Rockwell International
Mancheski, Frederick J.	Echlin Inc.
Merlis, Scott F.	Morgan Stanley & Company, Inc.
Miller, Robert R.	Motor & Equipment Manufacturers Association
Moore, Dan T.	Dan T. Moore Company
Murray, Pierre C.	MacLean-Fogg
Oakley, Thomas G.	Tenneco Automotive
Page, Robert T.	Parker Hannifin Corporation
Plumley, Michael A.	Plumley Companies, Inc.
Prechter, Heinz	ASC Incorporated
*Reilly, John P.	Brunswick Corporation
Reilly, J. Bernard	Eaton Corporation
Rilott, James H.	Atwood Industries, Inc.
Roland, David R.	Automotive Service Industry Association
Sebenius, James K.	Harvard University
Sights, Jack W.	Guardian Industries, Corp.
Singer, Richard J.	Singer Products
Tannehill, Jan E.	General Motors Corporation
Vignone, Rudolph A.	Goodyear Tire & Rubber Co.
Waterman, Richard C.	Anco Products Division, Cooper Industries
Zimmer, David R.	Core Industries Inc.
Bates, Christopher M.	Advisor

*Chairman of the Committee (formerly President & CEO of Tenneco Automotive)

TABLE OF CONTENTS

U.S.-JAPAN AUTO PARTS TRADE

FIVE YEARS AFTER

THE FAIR TRADE IN AUTO PARTS ACT

A Results Oriented Review

By the Auto Parts Advisory Committee

December 1993

FIVE YEAR REVIEW

Adopted as part of the Omnibus Trade and Competitiveness Act of 1988, the Fair Trade in Auto Parts Act established a five year initiative to improve access for U.S. made parts and accessories in Japanese original equipment (OE) and replacement parts markets including both Japan and the United States. The year 1993 marks both the five year point for that initiative and the beginning of the Clinton Administration's "Results Oriented", bilateral trade negotiations with Japan, under the United States-Japan Framework for a New Economic Partnership.

The automotive industries, including both the motor vehicle and the auto parts sectors, have been designated as major sectors under the Framework Negotiations. The joint statement issued in July 1993 by the President of the United States and the Prime Minister of Japan specifically stated that the bilateral government efforts "will have the objective, inter alia of achieving significantly expanded sales opportunities to result in a significant expansion of purchases of foreign parts by Japanese firms in Japan and through their transplants, as well as removing problems which affect market access, and encouraging imports of foreign autos and auto parts in Japan."

In November of 1993, Mr. Timothy J. Hauser, Acting Undersecretary of Commerce for International Trade, testified to Congress on the Framework Negotiations. Commenting on the auto parts sector of the Negotiations, Mr. Hauser stated that: "The United States Government has presented the Japanese with a comprehensive proposal that focuses on three main areas:

"Purchases of U.S. auto parts by Japanese transplant vehicle manufacturers,

Purchases of Foreign Auto Parts in Japan, and

Imports of Foreign Vehicles by Japan."

The U.S. proposal also "contains provisions for stronger enforcement of Japan's antitrust laws with respect to the Japanese automotive industry."

The Framework Negotiations and the U.S. objectives for the auto parts sector are consistent with the stated objectives of the new administrations in the United States and Japan. The Clinton Administration was elected on a platform that called for revitalization of the domestic economy in the United States, expanding exports, and guiding the post Cold War transition of persons employed in the military and defense industry to civilian employment. The Hosokawa Administration was elected on a platform of political reform and transforming the export oriented Japanese economy to a more consumer oriented economy.

The motor vehicle and auto parts industries are essential to the health of the American economy. Expansion of job opportunities for American workers and expansion of business opportunities for American owners and stockholders of auto parts companies are essential to any program to grow the American economy. Preservation and strengthening of the technological capabilities existing in the American motor vehicle and auto parts industries are essential as the foundation for technology transfer to other manufacturing industries having significant growth potential for the American economy.

No other economic sectors in the United States have anywhere near the potential of the motor vehicle and auto parts industries to grow through increased exports and displacement of imports to accomplish the domestic economic recovery and defense conversion goals of the Clinton Administration and the Congress. The Commerce Department has estimated that employment in the automotive and allied industries totals six million persons, or six percent of non-farm employment in the U.S. economy. Manufacturing employment in the automotive and allied industries is one million persons, equal to approximately seven percent of total manufacturing employment in the U.S.

The U.S. auto industry provides high value-added jobs generating about $100,000 value added per employee compared with an overall average for the entire U.S. economy of $48,000. The U.S. industry provides its employees with well above average pay, health benefits, and pension benefits.

The traditional sector of the industry accounts for about eleven percent of corporate R&D and employs approximately six percent of all scientists and engineers.

Over 5,000 U.S. owned companies conduct substantial business in the industry.

The U.S. auto parts manufacturing industry is a diverse $100 billion industry, directly employing over 700,000 people. Millions of other jobs are dependent on the results of the U.S. auto parts manufacturing industry. Exports of U.S. auto parts have grown over 60 percent since 1988, accounting for approximately $28.5 billion in U.S. exports in 1992.

Although the United States annually runs a trade deficit in auto parts, the gap between imports and exports has been closing every year since 1989, when the deficit was $14.5 billion. The 1992 gap was $5 billion. Since 1989, the United States actually has run an overall trade surplus in auto parts each year, except for the large trade deficit with Japan. The deficit with Japan was $9.8 billion in 1992, compared with $8.8 billion in 1988. For 1993, the bilateral trade deficit with Japan is expected to grow to a record $11 billion. This will reverse the last several years trend toward annual improvements in the U.S.'s overall auto parts trade performance. Studies for APAC by the Office for the Study of Automotive Transportation of the University of Michigan Transportation Research Institute project that the auto parts deficit with Japan will likely remain at current very high levels or worsen during the next several years.

The trade deficits with Japan and accompanying economic dislocations in the United States are persistent despite dramatic and well documented improvements in the competitiveness of the American auto parts industry, especially in the areas which the Japanese vehicle manufacturers have traditionally stated were the critical factors in selection of suppliers - price, quality, and deliverability--and despite American industry leadership in the newest high technology areas such as airbags, antilock braking systems, and lightweight materials. The trade deficit is growing despite dramatic changes in the Yen-Dollar ratios in recent years, which have favored U.S. manufactured products. The Yen-Dollar ratio is 109:1 in 1993 compared to 128:1 in 1988.

In the five years since the enactment of the Fair Trade in Auto Parts Act, the American government and industry have conducted numerous studies of the competitiveness of the U.S. auto parts industry and of the barriers to trade with the Japanese in both the original equipment markets and the aftermarkets in the U.S. and in Japan. The problems confronted by traditional U.S. manufacturers are numerous and well documented. (A list of major studies is presented in the Bibliography section of this report and the studies' findings are summarized in other sections of this and previous APAC Annual Reports).

U.S. auto parts manufacturers and their employees have experienced serious economic dislocation due to the lack of meaningful access to the Japanese market and to structural barriers which limit access to Japanese subsidiaries and affiliates in North America and key emerging automotive markets in developing countries.

The exclusionary practices of Japanese "keiretsu" groups linking vehicle and parts manufacturers in Japan and the United States continue to make it very difficult for U.S. auto parts suppliers to expand business with Japanese auto makers in all major world markets, despite U.S. industry competitiveness.

To help alleviate such problems and develop better working relationships, American and Japanese industry executives have conducted numerous company-to-company meetings and a variety of seminars and industry-to-industry meetings in recent years, including:

Annual "One-on-One"© meeting sessions between U.S. suppliers and Japanese vehicle manufacturers.

Annual "Design-In" Seminars

Overseas Supplier meetings

JAMA-MEMA Liaison Committee meetings

U.S. supplier participation in the Tokyo Motor Show

Since 1988, the United States and Japanese Governments also have conducted a variety of bilateral trade negotiations which have sought to increase trade and identify and rectify both generic trade barriers and auto sector specific trade barriers, including:

Market-Oriented Sector Selective Transportation Machinery Talks (MOSS)

Market-Oriented Cooperation Plan (MOCP)

Structural Impediments Initiative (SII)

Auto Parts Sector Negotiations under the Framework Agreement

The last five years of negotiations are not the first wave of bilateral, U.S.-Japan negotiations on auto parts. The first negotiations were the 1981-1983 U.S.-Japan Trade Facilitation Committee Negotiations on Auto Parts, which were actually terminated in 1981 at Japan's insistence. That was followed in 1985-1986 by the renewed Trade Facilitation Committee Negotiations. Those efforts evolved into the MOSS, MOCP, and SII efforts, which in 1993 evolved into the current Framework Negotiations.

A significant advance in the efforts to increase trade in auto parts occurred in January of 1992 when Prime Minister Miyazawa and President Bush announced their nations' commitments to the Global Partnership and the Global Partnership Plan of Action. That Plan of Action included descriptions of the Japanese car companies' "voluntary purchase plans" for U.S. auto parts, as follows:

- **Automobile parts procurement by U.S. manufacturing facilities of Japanese affiliates from U.S. suppliers is expected to more than double from about $7 billion in FY 1990 to about $15 billion (in real terms) in FY 1994.**

- **Seen in terms of percentage of local procurement in the total purchase of parts, the percentage is expected to increase from about 50% in FY 1990 to** about 70% in FY 1994. By contrast, the percentage of imports from Japan is expected to decrease from about 50% to 30%.

- In making these procurements, special consideration will be given to the U.S. parts industry.

- As for Japanese import of parts from the United States, it is expected to double from 2 billion dollars in FY 1990 to 4 billion dollars (in real terms) in FY 1994.

- In sum, the total local procurement in the United States and export to Japan (import by Japan), i.e. total purchase of U.S. parts will increase by about 10 billion dollars -from about 9 billion dollars in FY 1990 to about 19 billion dollars in FY 1994.

The Japanese-U.S. Action Plan includes the following discussion of the aggregated figures of the Japanese car companies' announcements:

-- will further strengthen such efforts as:

- promoting design-in (332 ongoing cases and 271 successfully completed cases as of January 1991);

- expanding R&D centers in the U.S. (7 centers of 6 firms with 1,400 employees, expected to increase to 2,200 employees in the near future); and

- assisting U.S. parts suppliers to develop long-term business relationships.

The figures in the Japanese voluntary plans are calculated using the data collected by the Japan Automobile Manufacturers Association (JAMA) pursuant to the MOSS agreement. The MOSS data differ from U.S. Commerce Department data on exports and imports by wide margins due to such factors as JAMA's inclusion of materials, insurance, freight, trading house margins, and other costs in its MOSS data. Purchases from traditional U.S. auto parts manufacturers and Japanese transplant manufacturing facilities are lumped together to make up the "American" supplier group. The MOSS data for several years and the voluntary plan year of JFY 1994 are presented here for comparison, to show the growth in reported purchases by Japanese vehicle manufacturers.

<u>1988</u>	<u>1990</u>	<u>1992</u>	<u>1994 Plans</u>
$4.9b	$9.1b	$13.6b	$19b

This growth in Japanese purchases of U.S. auto parts will be accomplished, in part, as a result of increases in Japanese vehicle production in the United States. Japanese vehicle production is projected to grow from the 1988 level of 882,000 units to 2,270,000 units in 1994.

The government and industry efforts which culminated in the Japanese-U.S. Action Plan's JFY 1994 parts purchase goals set the stage for substantial progress to be made in the current U.S.-Japan Framework Negotiations if both the U.S. and Japanese Governments are truly committed and remain persistent in their efforts to resolve trade issues and remove trade barriers.

Major improvements in U.S.-Japan auto parts trade remain to be accomplished. Even if the 1994 voluntary plans are met by the Japanese vehicle manufacturers, which remains in doubt, the Japanese transplant vehicle manufacturing operations in the United States are projected to utilize imported parts for 30 percent of total parts purchases. Total auto parts imports from Japan exceed $10 billion per year. The JAMA 1994 voluntary plans did not break out purchases from traditional vs. transplant suppliers in the U.S. However, according to a JAMA report, traditional U.S. suppliers currently supply an estimated 26 percent of the transplants' parts purchases, with over half of the Japanese transplant vehicle manufacturers' U.S. parts purchases coming from the increasing number of Japanese transplant parts suppliers. In Japan, imported parts still account for less than two percent of the over $160 billion auto parts and accessories market.[1]

Two years have passed since the Japanese government and vehicle manufacturers announced their voluntary plans for JFY 1994. No such announcements have been made for JFY 1995 or JFY 1996. Nor have other significant achievements been made in bilateral auto parts negotiations with Japan in the past two years.

The United States cannot afford to repeat the mistake of the early 1980's, when bilateral trade negotiations with Japan on auto parts were abandoned. In 1980, the U.S. had obtained Japanese agreement as part of a "results-oriented" negotiation to eliminate the $1 billion annual trade deficit beginning with a target of $300 million in Japanese imports of auto parts from the U.S. by 1981. The Trade Facilitation Committee negotiations were terminated in 1981, however, at Japan's insistence--two years earlier than previously agreed. Exports of U.S. auto parts did not reach the $300 million level until seven years later in 1988. In the meantime, the auto parts trade deficit with Japan had grown from $1 billion in 1980 to $8.8 billion.

---

[1]Note: In an "Industry Sector Analysis" prepared in September 1993, the U.S. and Foreign Commercial Service Office of the American Embassy in Tokyo, Japan estimated the 1991 local production in Japan at $159,772 million.

Regrettably, the Hosokawa Government's response to the Clinton Administration's auto and auto parts sector proposals under the Framework Negotiations in the fall of 1993 has been very disappointing. Acting Undersecretary Hauser testified on November 8, 1993 that:

> **"Thus far in the negotiations, the Government of Japan has put forth a number of arguments with respect to the automotive sector. They have stated that Japanese industry cannot make additional commitments at this time due to the depressed state of the industry. They have called for a two-way dialogue in this initiative which includes looking at the sales efforts and product quality of U.S. companies. They have also stated that these negotiations must be limited to actions within the scope and responsibility of the governments."**

The reaction of the Japan Automobile Manufacturers Association has been even more negative. In a press release dated November 8, 1993, JAMA strongly rejected the U.S. Government's proposals for the automotive and auto parts sectors as part of the Framework negotiations, stating:

> **"U.S. negotiators in the trade 'framework' talks with Japan are making demands that are 'shockingly discriminatory and anti-market,' according to the Japan Automobile Manufacturers Association (JAMA)."**

The Japan Automobile Manufacturers Association and the Government of Japan have criticized the United States Government's proposals for the automotive and auto parts sectors of the Framework Negotiations based upon a variety of points, but particularly the following:

(1) The activities of Japanese automotive companies relative to purchases of auto parts from U.S. Suppliers are business activities largely outside the responsibility of governments.

(2) The Japanese Government cannot agree to actions which would amount to "setting the expectation of governments" for Japanese automotive company purchases of U.S. auto parts or to "encouraging private companies to extend numerical projections beyond 1994" for purchases of U.S. auto parts because those projections might be considered as, or might become, targets to actually be achieved.

(3) Japanese vehicle manufacturers' purchases of auto parts from Japanese transplant companies in the U.S. should be considered by the U.S. Government as purchases of U.S. parts, the same as purchases from traditional U.S. auto parts companies.

76-349 O - 95 - 3

The negotiators for the Government of Japan have informed U.S. Government negotiators that Japan's primary interest in the Framework Negotiations on automobiles and auto parts is to obtain information on the export efforts of U.S. parts and vehicle manufacturers and on the efforts of U.S. parts companies to sell to the Japanese transplants in the U.S.

The opportunities that currently exist for growth in employment, ownership and technological capabilities in the U.S. motor vehicle and auto parts industries and the associated benefits to the United States economy and the American public need to be achieved. But those benefits can be achieved only if the United States and Japanese governments implement policies to effectively and expeditiously remove the already well documented barriers to increased exports of American made auto parts to Japan and to increased sales of American made auto parts to the Japanese transplant motor vehicle industry in the U.S.

The Auto Parts Advisory Committee has made an extensive and cohesive set of Policy Recommendations to the Secretary of Commerce for actions to increase trade with Japan in the U.S. and in the Japanese domestic market. The Policy Recommendations have been reviewed and updated during 1993 and are applicable to the current Framework Negotiations.

The Auto Parts Advisory Committee supports a strong, results-oriented U.S. Government position in the U.S.- Japan Framework Negotiations on auto parts trade. APAC also supports extension of the Fair Trade in Auto Parts Act, which was requested of Congress by the Clinton Administration in October, 1993. The U.S. Government's trade efforts must be persistent and the close industry-government cooperation (which has been exceptionally strong since the establishment of APAC) must continue if the U.S. government and U.S. auto parts industry are to achieve their mutual objectives for economic growth, high-quality employment, competition-based business opportunities and leading-edge technological advances that historically have provided enormous benefits to the American people in our consumer-oriented economy.

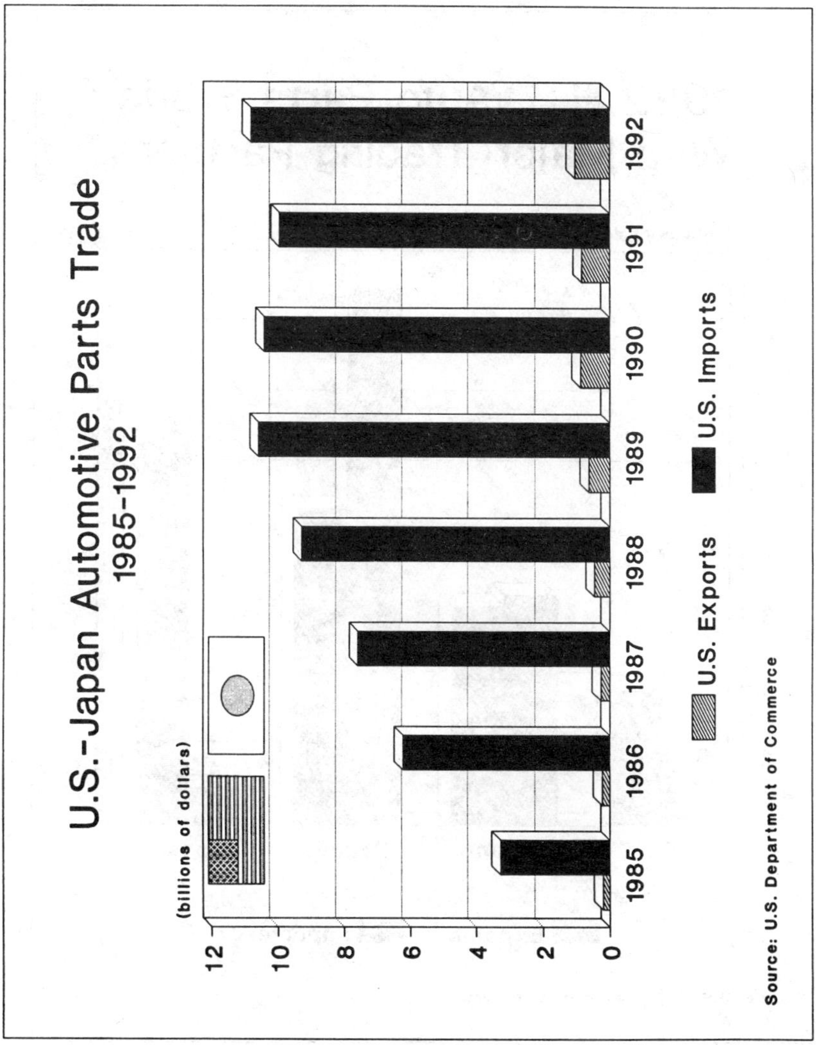

U.S.-Japan Automotive Parts Trade
1985-1992
(billions of dollars)
12
10
8
6
4
2
0
1985
1986
1987
1988
1989
1990
1991
1992
U.S. Exports
U.S. Imports
Source: U.S. Department of Commerce

1992 U.S. Auto Parts Trade With Major Trading Partners

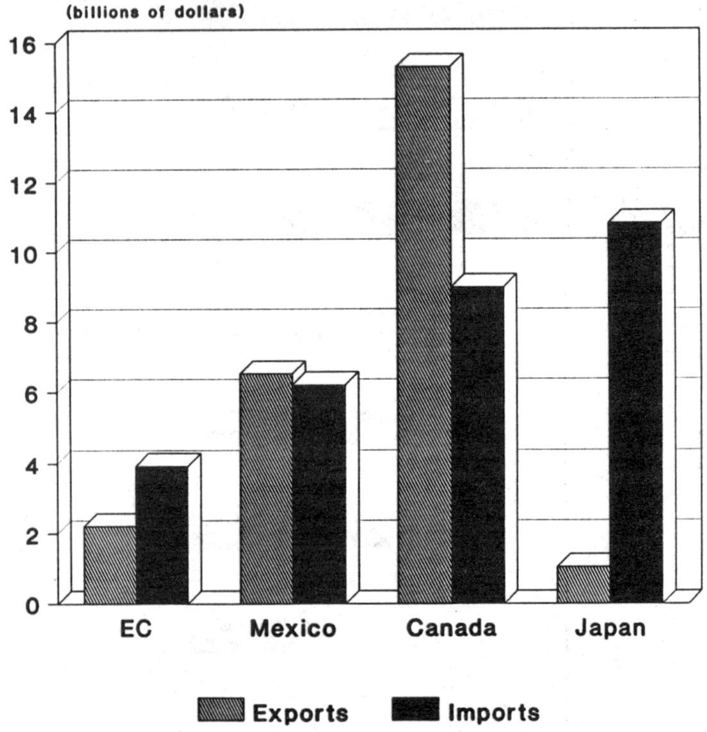

Source: U.S. Department of Commerce

Profile of the U.S. Automotive Parts Industry

SIC Code*	Number of Establishments	Employment (thousands)	Shipments ($ millions)	Value-Added ($ millions)	New Capital Expenditures ($ millions)
3465					
1990		110.6	14,544.5	6,300.2	912.4
1989		115.7	15,625.7	6,713.8	827.9
1987	713	119.8	15,251.6	6,659.3	1,285.0
1983	668	96.6	8,777.4	4,114.4	465.0
1977	591	138.0	9,739.2	4,654.5	292.2
3592					
1990		20.6	2,042.4	1,045.8	87.9
1989		21.8	2,265.5	1,160.1	71.8
1987	155	21.7	2,287.4	1,198.0	104.9
1983	171	29.8	2,224.5	1,385.1	106.0
1977	151	23.1	1,400.6	924.9	79.9
3647					
1990		14.9	2,121.7	1,025.1	103.5
1989		15.7	2,179.1	1,051.7	79.8
1987	72	14.4	1,969.6	957.1	75.7
1983	84	13.9	1,013.6	602.4	43.8
1977	75	21.6	908.5	536.0	46.3
3691					
1990		23.1	3,625.8	1,718.8	126.5
1989		24.5	3,358.5	1,580.7	119.4
1987	190	24.2	3,303.1	1,705.1	111.7
1983	201	22.4	2,431.3	1,203.0	109.7
1977	218	28.8	1,982.5	927.8	122.2
3694					
1990		46.1	5,810.5	2,846.7	197.2
1989		29.3	8,517.0	3,920.3	271.0
1987	486	67.3	7,472.6	3,432.4	237.7
1983	433	46.6	3,464.3	1,851.5	78.4
1977	409	57.5	3,647.2	2,041.3	146.0
3714					
1990		388.7	64,875.4	26,871.4	3,446.0
1989		393.3	65,682.8	26,458.4	2,964.0
1987	2,747	389.6	60,696.5	25,896.0	2,284.1
1983	2,420	338.0	36,293.1	16,764.6	1,791.7
1977	2,623	450.0	35,750.8	16,263.8	1,833.2
TOTA					
1990	4,000	604.0	93,020.3	39,808.0	4,873.5
1989	4,200	600.3	97,628.6	40,885.0	4,333.9
1987	4,363	637.0	90,980.8	39,847.9	4,099.1
1983	3,977	547.3	54,204.2	25,921.0	2,594.6
1977	4,067	719.0	53,428.8	25,348.3	2,519.8

Note: Actual data for the 1989 and 1990 number of establishments have not yet bee published. Total figures are estimated by DOC.

*SIC 3465: Automotive stampings
SIC 3592: Carburetors, pistons, piston rings and valves
SIC 3647: Vehicular lighting equipment
SIC 3691: Storage batteries
SIC 3694: Engine electrical equipment
SIC 3714: Motor vehicle parts and accessories

Source: Annual Survey of Manufactures, Census of Manufactures

APAC POLICY RECOMMENDATIONS

During 1993 the Auto Parts Advisory Committee (APAC) updated policy recommendations previously approved in April 1991 and adopted new policies and advice in support of results-oriented U.S.-Japan parts trade negotiations. The following actions were taken in May, September and November of 1993.

MAY 1993

AUTO PARTS ADVISORY COMMITTEE (APAC) BACKGROUND AND RECOMMENDATIONS ON U.S.-JAPAN TRADE EXECUTIVE SUMMARY

Background

The U.S. auto parts manufacturing industry has become fully cost and quality competitive on a global basis as a result of significant industry restructuring and favorable exchange rate shifts since the mid-1980s. However, the Japanese approach to world trade continues to be fundamentally and systematically out of sync with practices of all other major U.S. trading partners. Japanese business practices in the auto parts industry are increasing the U.S. bilateral trade deficit and causing serious economic dislocation in the United States.

- **The U.S. auto parts manufacturing sector is a diverse, $100 billion industry, with 4,000 firms directly employing over 700,000 people. Millions of other jobs and thousands of other businesses are dependent on the health of the U.S. auto parts manufacturing industry.**

- **U.S. industry is competitive internationally, as evidenced by its $26.5 billion in total exports, up more than 50% since 1988. Except for Japan, the U.S. had a $3.8 billion auto parts trade surplus with the rest of the world in 1992.**

- **The U.S.-Japan trade problem is principally an auto and auto parts problem. Last year, 63% of the rising U.S. trade deficit with Japan was automotive-related; 20% was in auto parts alone. At nearly $10 billion in 1992, the auto parts deficit with Japan grew ten-fold in the 1980s and is again rising.**

- **U.S. auto parts manufacturers and their employees have experienced serious economic dislocation due to the lack of meaningful access to the Japanese market and to structural barriers which limit access to Japanese subsidiaries and affiliates in North America and key emerging automotive markets in developing countries.**

- **The exclusionary practices of Japanese "keiretsu" groups linking vehicle and parts manufacturers in Japan and the United States continue to make it very**

difficult for U.S. auto parts suppliers to expand business with Japanese auto makers in all major world markets, despite U.S. industry competitiveness.

- **The Japanese market remains closed despite the negative impact on consumers. The U.S. Department of Commerce in 1991 released results of a joint U.S.-Japanese government survey which showed retail auto parts prices in Japan in many cases are from 200% to 300% higher than in the United States.**

- **Several recent studies show that the U.S. auto parts industry is significantly more cost competitive then its Japanese counterparts in the original equipment supply business.**

Recommendations

APAC strongly requests that the Administration designate the U.S. auto parts industry as a "Strategic Export Sector" in the Bilateral Framework Negotiations to be undertaken by the U.S. and Japanese Governments. This request is contained in the attached APAC policy recommendations, which are an integrated package. This paper also outlines four principal objectives for dramatically improving the balance in the U.S.-Japan auto parts trading relationship. APAC urges the U.S. Government to:

1) **Continue to insist on achievement of the Japanese U.S. parts purchasing and local content targets with special emphasis on traditional U.S. suppliers set for fiscal year 1994;**

2) **Take other interim steps -including opening the original equipment and aftermarket in Japan to U.S. suppliers and continuous improvements in expanded purchases and design-in relationships with U.S. suppliers in North America, necessary to reach an equitable and sustainable auto parts trade relationship with Japan by 1998;**

3) **These actions should facilitate agreement with the Japanese Government, in cooperation with U.S. and Japanese industry, to achieve major annual reductions in the massive and growing U.S. auto parts trade deficit with Japan over a five-year period to a level which reflects U.S. industry's strong international competitive position and is consistent with other major U.S. bilateral trading relationships; and**

4) **Monitor, in cooperation with U.S. industry on a regular basis, the progress which non-Japanese affiliated U.S. automotive suppliers are making in expanding original equipment and aftermarket sales and business relationships with Japanese companies in the United States and Japan.**

The APAC also recommends a series of reinforcing U.S. Government policy actions, including, but not limited to:

- **Extension of the Fair Trade in Auto Parts Act for five years;**

- **Congressional approval of U.S. implementing legislation on the North American Free Trade Agreement with appropriate supplemental agreements;**

- **Extension of "fast track" authority to facilitate completion and congressional approval of the GATT Uruguay Round;**

- **Full implementation of newly issued Commerce Department regulations on foreign-trade zones; and**

- **Expansion of U.S. Government data collection and analysis related to U.S.-Japanese auto parts trade and Japanese investment in the United States.**

I. POLICY PHILOSOPHY

APAC strongly supports open markets for motor vehicles and auto parts, in which success is achievable through fair and open competition among manufacturers. APAC members are confident that the U.S. auto parts industry can successfully compete in every automotive market in the world if competition is not restricted by non-market barriers or exclusionary practices either imposed or tolerated by national governments. APAC's focus is on: "markets, including those in the United States and Japan, where automotive parts and accessories, both original equipment and aftermarket are purchased for use in the manufacture or repair of Japanese automobiles," as stated in the Fair Trade in Auto Parts Act of 1988.

APAC strongly recommends that prompt removal of such barriers and exclusionary practices must be a major objective of the U.S. government if the new Administration is to achieve the important goals of an expanded domestic economy and reduced trade deficit for the United States. Effective export promotion should continue to be an important complement to market opening initiatives.

APAC also recommends that government programs to intervene in markets only be utilized when the government's efforts to open markets and facilitate trade, through such actions as effective application of U.S. trade, investment and competition policies have not been successful in assuring fair opportunities for U.S. companies. APAC concludes that the evidence proves this to be the case with respect to U.S. government efforts to open markets and facilitate trade in auto parts with Japan. Numerous government and private studies in recent years have documented the unjustifiable and unacceptable imbalances in auto

parts trade with Japan and the exclusionary nature of the Japanese markets. The U.S. auto parts industry and the U.S. government have repeatedly emphasized the necessity of eliminating market barriers and achieving steady improvements in actual business.

APAC continues to emphasize that success in market opening activities must be measured in actual trade, sales and business relationships. APAC is committed to increased private sector and government efforts to accelerate the pace of accomplishment in opening Japanese auto parts markets.

II. SUPPORT FOR ADMINISTRATION REVIEW OF TRADE POLICY OPTIONS

APAC supports the new Administration's review of the trade performance of foreign countries and openness of their domestic markets and of the options for U.S. actions (including U.S. government self-initiation of trade actions such as anti-dumping, section 301, and proposed Super 301 extension) against countries which are not living up to their fair trade obligations as major participants in the global auto parts market and/or are maintaining closed domestic markets.

APAC strongly requests that the Administration designate the U.S. auto parts industry as a "Strategic Export Sector" in the Bilateral Framework Negotiations to be undertaken by the U.S. and Japanese Governments. The industry clearly merits this designation, given its world-class competitive capability, massive economic and trade significance, and position as a primary generator and user of advanced technology.

APAC is committed to working constructively with the U.S. government as representatives of the U.S. auto parts industry to provide reliable information and accurate and pragmatic advice during that review. Policy options that are considered should include identification of the measurable results which are expected. APAC strongly believes that options adopted for U.S. implementation must be results-oriented.

III. SUPPORT FOR RESULTS ORIENTED APPROACH

APAC strongly recommends that the U.S. auto parts industry be designated as a "Strategic Export Sector" in the Bilateral Framework Negotiations to be undertaken by the U.S. and Japanese Governments.

The U.S. auto parts trade deficit with Japan continues to grow despite the global cost and quality competitiveness of U.S. industry, major cooperative business development initiatives by U.S. and Japanese industry and government, and large favorable exchange rate shifts since the mid-1980s. Progress is being made, but not at a rate commensurate with U.S. producers' efforts and competitive capability. Unless much faster progress is made, economic dislocation in U.S. industry will increase and the already huge U.S. auto parts trade deficit with Japan will deteriorate further.

APAC supports past U.S. Government activities to open Japanese auto parts markets and increase U.S. auto parts exports to Japan through the Structural Impediments Initiative (SII) and the Market-Oriented Sector Selective (MOSS) talks on transportation equipment, including the Market-Oriented Cooperation Plan (MOCP) established in mid-1991. These programs represent important, but insufficient steps toward removal of Japanese barriers to increased U.S. auto parts exports, and toward establishment of effective long-term business relationships between U.S. suppliers and Japanese vehicle producers on a global basis.

To accelerate progress, APAC urges the U.S. Government to undertake additional market opening initiatives to complement ongoing U.S. industry efforts to expand auto parts sales and exports to Japanese producers. APAC supports a results-oriented approach to auto parts trade negotiations with Japan. The primary goal of this approach should be to establish a reasonable, measurable, and enforceable set of market-based results which would be considered a "successful outcome" in terms of future auto parts negotiations with Japan.

APAC strongly recommends that the U.S. Government:

(1) Continue to insist on achievement of the Japanese U.S. parts purchasing and local content targets with special emphasis and traditional U.S. suppliers set for fiscal year 1994;

(2) Take other interim steps -including opening the original equipment and aftermarket in Japan to U.S. suppliers and continuous improvements in expanded purchases and design-in relationships with U.S. suppliers in North America- necessary to reach an equitable and sustainable auto parts trade relationship with Japan by 1998;

(3) These actions should facilitate agreement with the Japanese Government, in cooperation with U.S. and Japanese industry, to achieve major annual reductions in the massive and growing U.S. auto parts trade deficit with Japan over a five-year period to a level which reflects U.S. industry's strong international competitive position and is consistent with other major U.S. bilateral trading relationships; and

(4) Monitor, in cooperation with U.S. industry on a regular basis, the progress which non-Japanese affiliated U.S. automotive suppliers are making in expanding original equipment and aftermarket sales and business relationships with Japanese companies in the United States and Japan.

APAC is committed to working closely with the U.S. Government to define appropriate measurable results, timetables, monitoring mechanisms, and enforcement options to achieve these goals and the broader objectives of the U.S.-Japan Bilateral Framework Agreement.

IV. FAIR TRADE IN AUTO PARTS ACT EXTENSION

APAC supports the five-year extension of the Fair Trade in Auto Parts Act (FTAPA) beyond its scheduled expiration at the end of 1993. APAC also stands ready to assist the Department of Commerce and Congress with advice on appropriate enhancements for the extended statute.

V. FAST TRACK AUTHORITY FOR NEGOTIATION OF GENERAL AGREEMENT ON TARIFFS AND TRADE (GATT)

APAC supports extension of Fast Track authority for conclusion of agreements for the current round of GATT negotiations.

APAC opposes proposals advanced by other countries in the GATT and other trade negotiations to weaken U.S. laws including, but not necessarily limited to anti-dumping and countervailing duties, section 301 and section 337. APAC also opposes any GATT measure that would alter U.S. industrial design law.

VI. NORTH AMERICAN FREE TRADE AGREEMENT (NAFTA)

APAC supports U.S. ratification of the North American Free Trade Agreement (NAFTA) and implementation of the agreement by January 1, 1994.

APAC wishes to be briefed and consulted by the U.S. government during negotiations of proposed supplemental agreements to the NAFTA on environmental protection, labor rights and standards, and import surges. These agreements could have significant impact on the U.S. auto parts industry. These agreements must be designed to: 1) promote harmonization of North American automotive industry standards along lines consistent with the interests of U.S producers and 2) avoid harm to U.S. automotive producers or their employees.

All side agreements should be made fully public.

VII. FOREIGN-TRADE ZONES

APAC supports full implementation of the current Foreign-Trade Zones (FTZ) rules, including the review provisions, to achieve the significant public benefits required for all subzone operations as measured by the public interest criteria specified in the rules.

VIII. CORPORATE AVERAGE FUEL ECONOMY PROGRAM (CAFE)

APAC recognizes that the structure and implementation of the U.S. Corporate Average Fuel Economy Program (CAFE), particularly the provisions related to different treatment of the domestic and import fleets and the domestic content requirements, can affect the market share of U.S. and Japanese nameplate vehicles, and the automotive parts trade between the U.S. and Japan.

APAC urges the Administration and Congress to consider the opportunities afforded U.S. parts suppliers to supply Japanese and U.S. nameplate vehicle manufacturers in any proposed revision to the CAFE law or regulations. Any changes should be designed to avoid harm to U.S. suppliers' ability to expand sales to Japanese auto makers or potential shifts of some of U.S. suppliers' traditional business with the big three to foreign parts manufacturers.

IX. DATA COLLECTION AND ANALYSIS

APAC supports expansion of government and private sector programs for the collection and analysis of accurate data related to auto parts trade with Japan to assure improvement of trade opportunities. APAC also supports full implementation of the Foreign Direct Investment and International Financial Data Improvement Act of 1990, including the Congressionally mandated priority for auto parts data, and reporting provisions for foreign-owned corporations in the Omnibus Budget Reconciliation Act of 1990. APAC supports promulgation of rules fully implementing the American Automobile Labelling Act in a manner which maximizes consistency with the cost and value-added measurement and reporting requirements of the CAFE program and NAFTA agreement.

APAC recognizes that limitations on data availability and applicability exist in many areas of U.S.-Japanese trade in auto parts. APAC cautions data users to consider this fact when reviewing or using such data.

APAC strongly supports prompt completion of the International Trade Commission's study of Japanese and U.S. investment in the ASEANs, Korea and Taiwan, including trade effects on U.S. and Japanese auto parts trade with these countries. Each of these countries have or are developing significant automotive vehicle and parts manufacturing industries.

X. U.S. RESEARCH, DEVELOPMENT AND TECHNOLOGY ASSISTANCE PROGRAMS

APAC recommends that United States Government agencies, including the Department of Energy, Department of Commerce, Department of Defense, and Environmental Protection Agency, adopt regulations requiring that foreign companies which participate in or receive the results of research and development or other technology programs provide continuing

assurances that their procurement and sales practices do not discriminate against U.S. auto parts suppliers.

XI. GOVERNMENT INVESTMENT INCENTIVES

APAC recommends that the Federal Government review its economic development grant programs and initiate discussions with state governments to encourage the states to adopt and implement policies to:

- **provide better balance between investment related incentive programs, including employee training programs, available to modernization projects and incentives available to greenfield projects,**
- **provide better balance between programs to promote exports and those to attract inward investment,**
- **require that companies which receive investment incentives provide continuing assurances that their procurement and sales practices do not discriminate against U.S. auto parts suppliers.**

APAC further recommends that model state laws and regulations be developed to implement such policies.

XII. REVIEW OF ANTI-DISCRIMINATION POLICIES

APAC requests the Department of Justice, in cooperation with other federal agencies, to review the applicability of federal anti-discrimination laws and regulations to allegations of discrimination against companies operating in the U.S. to assure that such companies do not discriminate in their employment and procurement practices against U.S. citizens.

SEPTEMBER 1993
SUPPORT FOR NEW PARTS TRADE NEGOTIATIONS

APAC Adopted the following resolution at its September 9, 1993 meeting.

The Auto Parts Advisory Committee (APAC) commends the Administration's significant accomplishment in obtaining Japan's agreement to designate the U.S. auto parts and auto industries as a major sector for market access negotiations to be undertaken under the United States-Japan Framework for a New Economic Partnership.

Important new elements for "results oriented" negotiations provided for by the Framework, including timetables and goals, fully meet the primary objective set in APAC's May 1993 recommendation, that the new negotiating approach should allow for establishment of a

reasonable, measurable and enforceable set of market based results which would be considered a successful outcome in terms of future auto parts negotiations with Japan.

APAC strongly urges that the Administration fully draw upon the unique negotiating authority conferred by the Fair Trade in Auto Parts Act, to address "Japanese market" barriers both in the U.S. and Japan. The Act's mandate is to foster increased access for U.S.-made auto parts in "Japanese markets," defined as "markets including those in the United States and Japan, where automotive parts and accessories, both original equipment and aftermarket, are purchased for use in the manufacture or repair of Japanese automobiles."

APAC concludes that the Act's distinctive definition should support the Committee's previously recommended policy that increased access for U.S. parts producers in "Japanese markets" could be best measured in terms of the progress which non-Japanese owned or controlled U.S. automotive suppliers are making in expanding original equipment and aftermarket sales and business relationships with Japanese companies in the United States and Japan. The issue of monitoring progress is vital to the attainment of APAC's other principal objectives for dramatically improving the balance in the bilateral trade relationship.

APAC also supports the other negotiations and consultations initiated under the Framework to expand trade and remove structural impediments, which will assure a comprehensive approach to a broad array of issues including regulatory reform, competition policy, distribution, investment and others that intersect with specific sectoral concerns of U.S. auto parts makers seeking to expand sales and business relationships with Japanese auto companies in the United States and Japan.

APAC is confident that the highly competitive non-Japanese owned or controlled U.S. automotive supplier industry can achieve significant results in expanded trade, sales and business relationships with Japanese auto companies if non-market barriers and exclusionary practices are promptly removed. APAC also supports the Administration's determination to reserve its right to use Section 301 and other appropriate trade statutes if necessary.

NOVEMBER LETTER SUPPORTING NEGOTIATIONS

APAC

Auto
Parts
Advisory
Committee

November 9, 1993

The Honorable Ronald H. Brown
Secretary of Commerce
U.S. Department of Commerce
14th Street & Constitution Ave., NW
Washington, DC 20230

Dear Secretary Brown:

This letter is to reaffirm the position of the U.S. Department of Commerce Auto Parts Advisory Committee (APAC) which supports a strong, results-oriented U.S. Government position in the U.S. Japan Framework Negotiations on auto parts trade.

As you know, APAC adopted policy positions earlier this year requesting the U.S. Government include the U.S. auto parts industry as a Strategic Export Sector in the bilateral Framework Negotiations with Japan and urging the U.S. Government to "undertake additional market opening initiatives to complement ongoing U.S. industry efforts to expand auto parts sales and exports to Japanese producers" based upon the "results oriented" approach.

Recently, the U.S. press has published documents on the "Japanese Proposal for Auto Framework Agreement" (See Inside U.S. Trade, Special Report on October 29, 1993) and the "Arrangement Between the Government of Japan and the Government of the United States of America Concerning Trade in Automotive Goods" (See Inside U.S. Trade, Special Report, November 1, 1993). As reported, the Japanese proposal is clearly not consistent with the APAC policy positions. It does not include substantive market opening initiatives required to increase sales of U.S. auto parts to the Japanese producers either in the United States or Japan. The reported Japanese proposal therefore appears to reflect significant backsliding on market opening and trade reforms on the part of the current Japanese Government compared to the achievements the Government of Japan during the 1991-1992 auto parts trade negotiations, especially in terms of persuading the Japanese vehicle manufacturers to publicly announce their future model year goals for U.S. auto parts purchases.

The Honorable Ronald H. Brown
November 9, 1993
Page 2 of 2

APAC members continue to support the position that "the highly competitive non-Japanese owned or controlled U.S. automotive supplier industry can achieve significant results in expanded trade, sales and business relationships with Japanese auto companies if non-market barriers and exclusionary practices are properly removed." We urge the U.S. Government to push forward with the U.S. "Arrangement" proposals to open markets and achieve reasonable and measurable results.

Thank you,

J.P. Reilly
Chairman,
Auto Parts Advisory Committee

PRINCIPAL U.S. GOVERNMENT ACTIONS

Omnibus Trade and Competitiveness Act of 1988

The 1988 Trade Act (Public Law 100-410) contained several provisions relating to auto parts trade with the Japanese. One such provision, the Fair Trade in Auto Parts Act sponsored by then Senator Dan Quayle, requires the Secretary of Commerce to establish an Auto Parts Advisory Committee (APAC) to advise the Department on programs to increase sales of U.S.-made auto parts and accessories to Japanese automotive manufacturers worldwide. Section 2124 et seq. of the Trade Act requires APAC to:

(1) report to the Secretary of Commerce on barriers to sales of United States-made auto parts and accessories in Japanese markets;

(2) review and consider data collected on sales of United States-made auto parts and accessories in Japanese markets;

(3) advise the Secretary of Commerce during consultations with the Government of Japan on issues concerning sales of United States-made auto parts in Japanese markets;

(4) assist in establishing priorities for the initiative established under section 2123 and otherwise provide assistance and direction to the Secretary of Commerce in carrying out the intent of that section; and

(5) assist the Secretary in reporting, or otherwise report to the Congress as requested, on the progress of sales of United States-made auto parts in Japanese markets.

The Fair Trade in Auto Parts Act also requires the Secretary of Commerce to "establish an initiative to increase sales of United States-made auto parts and accessories to Japanese markets." "Japanese markets are defined" by the Act, as "markets including those in the United States and Japan, where automotive parts and accessories, both original equipment and aftermarket, are purchased for use in the manufacture or repair of Japanese automobiles." The statutory authorities for the Commerce initiative are broad and include actions to "foster increased access to facilitate the exchange of information . . . collect data and market information . . . facilitate contacts. . . attempt to resolve disparities, policies, or practices, whether public or private, that result in barriers . . . initiate periodic consultations with officials of the Government of Japan . . . and report annually to the Congress."

The 1988 Trade Act also includes a Sense of Congress resolution on the auto parts MOSS, Section 1934 of the Trade Act, stating in part:

> **"United States automotive parts producers meet increasingly rigorous requirements for quality, just-in-time supply, and competitive pricing in the United States market; and the market-oriented sector specific (MOSS) talks on auto parts are aimed at overcoming substantial market access barriers and increasing the access of United States auto parts producers to the original equipment and replacement parts market represented by Japanese automobiles produced in Japan, the United States, and third countries."**
>
> **The resolution goes on to state the Sense of Congress that:**
>
> **"Success of the MOSS talks will be measured by a significant increase in sales by United States auto parts companies and the initiation of long-term sourcing relationships between such companies."**

Section 1301 of the Trade Act permits Section 301 retaliation against a foreign government's toleration of an unfair practice, rather than solely against the government practice itself.

The Conference Report on the Trade Act explains this provision's new statutory authority for U.S. negotiators to address private practices, such as automotive industry structural impediments:

> **"This provision reflects the growing conviction on the part of the conferees that anti-competitive, market restrictive behavior on the part of private firms, when coupled with the failure of a foreign government to intervene to eliminate such behavior, can act as a barrier to market access which is an great as any formal government act, policy, or practice alone. This has been particularly evident in such sectors as automobile parts, soda ash and semiconductors."**

Section 1301 et seq., the "Super 301" provision in effect during 1989 and 1990, required USTR to identify priority countries and trade practices for negotiations to eliminate trade barriers and open selected foreign markets in 1989 and 1990. Included in Super 301's changes Section 301 was the requirement that USTR negotiate with each foreign country in question to eliminate the trade barriers within three years, or assure the U.S. of adequate compensation.

In October of 1993, the Clinton Administration formally requested that Congress extend the Fair Trade in Auto Parts Act and the statutory authority contained therein for the Auto Parts Advisory Committee until December 31, 1998.

THE TRADE EXPANSION ACT OF 1992 (H.R. 5100)

Passage of the Trade Expansion Act of 1992 by the House of Representatives on July 8, 1992 marked the year's most significant Congressional parts trade action. The legislation's important provisions affecting U.S. automotive suppliers included the following:

> **A required USTR self-initiated Section 301 investigation, and negotiation of an agreement with Japan, to eliminate or modify policies and practices including toleration of systematic anticompetitive activities such as Keiretsu relationships and exclusionary business practices, that act as barriers to U.S. vehicle and parts exports.**
>
> **Other elements to be secured by the agreement include the implementation and enforcement of prior Japanese commitments, the establishment of longer term goals for greater design-in cooperation, and the provision for exchange of sales data exchange measured in terms of sales by non-Japanese owned or controlled U.S. based parts makers.**
>
> **Five-year extension of the Fair Trade in Auto Parts Act from 1993-1998, thereby continuing the Japanese parts market opening initiative and the role of the Auto Parts Advisory Committee in assisting programs to increase sales of U.S.-made parts and accessories in Japanese vehicle equipment markets worldwide.**
>
> **Five-year extension (1993-1997) of Super 301 authority earlier provided by the 1988 trade act for calendar years 1989 and 1990. Super 301 requires USTR to identify annually those priority countries and trade practices for trade liberalization negotiations and initiation of Section 301 investigations.**
>
> **Required the Foreign Trade Zones (TFZ) Board to review operations of all motor vehicle and parts subzones to determine whether any subzones are not having a net positive effect on the U.S. economy, according to the standards of the Act and FTZ rules, and should possibly be revoked or modified.**
>
> **Mandated negotiations to conclude bilateral and multilateral agreements to eliminate adverse effects of private anticompetitive practices on trade, harmonize competition policies, and establish mechanisms to enforce trade related competition policies.**

The House also adopted the Gephardt-Levin amendment effectively codifying Japanese auto makers' voluntary sourcing goals for $19 billion in U.S. parts purchases and a 70% U.S. content level in their U.S. subsidiaries by JFY 1994.

AMERICAN AUTOMOBILE LABELING ACT

Information required under the new American Automobile Labeling Act (AALA), Section 210 of the Motor Vehicle Information and Cost Savings Act, will help gauge U.S. content levels in all vehicles sold here. Effective October 1, 1994 all passenger cars, MPVs and trucks will bear a content label showing: the percentage of U.S.-Canadian parts value, the source country for engines and transmissions, vehicle assembly point, and names of countries supplying 15 percent or more of total parts value.

The label's value as an industry and economic bellwether will be enhanced by a strict all-or-nothing content rule for outside (independent) suppliers; vehicle makers will be able to count as U.S.-Canadian parts value only those parts made by outside suppliers that are at least 70% U.S.-Canadian value. Thus, high levels of U.S.-Canadian parts value generally will show that U.S. suppliers and their subcontractors had a major stake in the critical high value-added parts and jobs used.

Congress ordered early rulemaking to facilitate voluntary compliance before October 1, 1994, and the National Highway Traffic Safety Administration (NHTSA) currently is undertaking a proposed rulemaking with the public comment period scheduled to close January 18, 1994.

NORTH AMERICAN FREE TRADE AGREEMENT (NAFTA)

Consistent with APAC's Policy Recommendation, Congress approved NAFTA implementing legislation in November 1993 and the Agreement's implementation will begin January 1, 1994. APAC's principal objectives for the Agreement and the Supplemental Side Agreements were met. NAFTA's benefits to U.S. automotive suppliers include ten-year removal of all tariff and non-tariff barriers on automotive and automotive parts trade and an automotive rule of origin with regional value content measured by net cost formula increasing from 50 percent (1994-97) to 56 percent (1998-2001) and ultimately to 62.5 percent in 2002. Other APAC-recommended provisions include investment liberalization and guaranteed national treatment and safeguards against import surges that might injure or threaten injury to U.S. producers and workers.

APAC agrees with the conclusion reached in the International Trade Administration Report on NAFTA opportunities for U.S. motor vehicle and parts makers:

> "U.S. exporters of automotive parts and motor vehicles are among the biggest beneficiaries of the North American Free Trade Agreement (NAFTA), which takes the Mexican automotive market from a state of heavy protection to free trade within 10 years."

GENERAL AGREEMENT ON TARIFFS AND TRADE (GATT)

The GATT Round was completed prior to the December 15 deadline imposed by the Fast Track Authority Extension passed by Congress in 1993. APAC had identified a number of key GATT issues for U.S. auto parts manufacturers including reduction of foreign tariff and non-tariff barriers and removal of foreign trade related investment measures such as local content and export performance requirements.

APAC specifically opposed any efforts under GATT to weaken U.S. trade laws including antidumping, countervailing duty, Section 301 and Section 337 trade remedies, and also opposed any GATT-forced alteration of U.S. industrial design law.

MINIVAN DUMPING CASE

In its May 1992 final determination that Toyota was dumping minivans, the International Trade Administration (ITA) made an innovative examination of Toyota's ties to its keiretsu suppliers. ITA found that Japanese suppliers charged lower prices for parts used in assembling export model vehicles than those used to build vehicles for sale in Japan.

According to the ITA ruling:

> **"We have determined that the transfer prices between Toyota and its related suppliers do not represent arm's length transactions within the meaning of section 773(e)(2) of the Act."**

Among ITA's reasons for adjusting the transfer prices reported by Toyota is the following:

> **"Despite Toyota's assertion, our analysis of the prices between Toyota and its related suppliers reveals that there is a systematic pattern of differences with respect to one element of the prices paid for parts and components used to produce the minivan sold in the home market and at the same element of the prices paid for parts and components used to produce the exported vehicles. Toyota has claimed that these differences are due to economic factors. We, however, have analyzed Toyota's claims for the cause of the observed differences and have found Toyota's explanations unconvincing when taken as a whole."**

No penalties were imposed because no injury determination was made by the International Trade Commission (ITC).

FOREIGN-TRADE ZONES

The Department of Commerce Foreign-Trade Zones (FTZ) Board issued new FTZ program rules on October 8, 1991 (effective November 7, 1991). The rule is comprehensive and constitutes a complete revision, replacing the present version of 15 CFR part 400. The Board's summary of the revised rule states that "the regulations are designed to make zone procedures reasonably accessible to qualified zone users without resulting in harmful consequences that are detrimental to the public interest."

The major changes involve the adoption of definitive "public interest" criteria and review procedures both for new zone applicants as well as the review and monitoring of existing subzone operations. According to the Board, "applicants for subzones must also demonstrate a significant public benefit" with the new public interest criteria "being a yardstick."

In the rule's background section, the Board observed that "there is growing concern about manufacturing activity in zones and subzones," which it describes as follows:

> "Firms interested in using zones for manufacturing seek greater access and flexibility in zone procedures to help them compete against imports of finished goods and increase their exports. Those opposing zone manufacturing operations contend that zone procedures should be more restrictive for non-export operations, especially when inverted tariffs (actual or effective lower duty rate on finished product) are involved.

Subsequent to the reform of FTZ program rules two applications for expansion of Japanese owned subzone assembly operations, opposed by the U.S. motor vehicle and parts industries, were approved by the Board in 1993.

FOREIGN DIRECT INVESTMENT AND INTERNATIONAL FINANCIAL DATA IMPROVEMENTS ACT OF 1990 DATA IMPROVEMENTS

President Bush signed the foreign Direct Investment and International Financial Data Improvements Act of 1990 (S. 2516) on November 7, 1990, establishing improved data systems that may help auto parts trade negotiations.

In his signing statement, the President said:

> "This Act requires the Secretary of Commerce to produce an annual report on the role and significance of foreign direct investment in the United States. The report will provide information with sufficient detail so that analysis of such investment in various industry sectors and geographic areas will be improved."

The House Energy and Commerce Committee report accompanying the House version of the bill (H.R. 4520) directs that the United States automotive supplier industry be one such sector to benefit from the improved analysis. According to the Committee's section-by-section analysis of the bill:

> **"The Committee notes that the Omnibus Trade and Competitiveness Act of 1988 (1988 Trade Act) established the Auto Parts Advisory Committee (APAC) to advise the Secretary of Commerce in auto parts negotiations. The APAC has in turn urged the Administration to utilize all relevant trade and investment data in formulating policy and negotiating positions.**
>
> **The exchange of information between the BEA and the Census under this section could be of immediate potential value of U.S. trade negotiators. Of particular relevance are the ongoing and critical U.S.-Japan negotiations to attain greater access for U.S. firms in the original equipment and replacement parts markets for vehicles built and sold by Japanese vehicle makers and their affiliates in the United States. The Committee urges priority attention to the exchange of that data with immediate utility for U.S. trade negotiators."**

ITC REPORT ON THIRD COUNTRY TRADE

Consistent with APAC's Policy Recommendation, The International Trade Commission (ITC) has agreed to study Japanese and U.S. investment in the ASEAN's, Korea and Taiwan. Issues for examination include trade effects on U.S. and Japanese auto parts trade with these countries. Each of the countries being studied have or are developing significant motor vehicle and parts-making industries.

MOSS DATA ON AUTO PARTS SALES TO JAPANESE VEHICLE PRODUCERS

Under the terms of the 1987 MOSS agreement on auto parts, the Japanese government agreed to provide the U.S. government with semi-annual statistics on aggregate purchases of U.S. auto parts collected by the Japan Automobile Manufacturers Association (JAMA). The semi-annual statistics were to be provided for five Japanese fiscal years (JFYs), JFY 1987 (April, 1987 - March, 1988) through JFY 1991 (April, 1991 - March, 1992). JAMA subsequently has continued its semi-annual reports as a means of reporting Japanese auto makers' parts purchases under their January 1992 announced voluntary sourcing goals.

JAMA data cover all purchases of production and service parts, accessories, and materials from U.S. suppliers, whether U.S. or foreign-owned, for use in the United States and Japanese markets. Separate data are provided for the following categories of purchases: engine parts, chassis and drivetrain parts, body parts, electrical and electronic parts, accessories, and materials. Table 2 shows the trend in reported JAMA member purchases from U.S. suppliers in each of these categories from JFY 1985 through JFY 1992, with half-year JFY 1993 data provided covering April 1 to September 30, 1993.

According to the JAMA data, total sales of U.S. auto parts to Japanese vehicle producers and their U.S. subsidiaries rose from $4.9 billion in JFY 1988 to $13.6 billion in JFY 1992, representing almost a 180 percent increase over four years. Half-year JFY 1993 purchase of $7.2 billion suggest annualized JFY 1993 purchases of $14.4 billion,[2] or roughly a 6 percent increase over JFY 1992 and a 195 percent increase over JFY 1988. To provide some context, U.S.-based assembly of Japanese designed vehicles increased from approximately 882,000 units in 1988, to nearly 1.8 million units in 1992 and 1993.

JAMA reports that over 80 percent of the $8.45 billion in total JFY 1991 purchases and $11.2 billion total JFY 1992 purchases were for use in the United States compared to $3.86 billion purchased for U.S. market use in JFY 1988. Respectively, $2.08 billion and $2.4 billion were purchased in JFY 1991 and JFY 1992 for export to Japan compared to $1.05 billion in JFY 1990 reported U.S. parts exports. Reported JFY 1992 imports of U.S. parts represented a 20 percent increase over JFY 1990's imports of $1.95 billion worth of U.S. parts.

The JAMA figures which form the MOSS data on imports to Japan are approximately two-and-one-half times the level reported in U.S. trade statistics ($826 million in 1991 and $1.035 billion in 1992). The MOSS data differs from Department of Commerce trade data by wide margins due to such factors as JAMA's inclusion of materials, insurance, freight, trading house margins, and other costs in their MOSS data.

---

[2]Note: Seasonal fluctuations could change this data.

JAMA statistics on purchases from U.S. suppliers, because they are highly aggregated, do not provide sufficient basis for assessing the progress of U.S. suppliers in selling to individual Japanese vehicle makers or their subsidiaries.

Although the JAMA statistics include purchases for aftermarket maintenance, repair and modification, they do not differentiate between original equipment (OE) and aftermarket parts purchases. This is of special concern, because the Big Five Japanese auto makers used the JFY 1990 JAMA data (which under MOSS agreement is to include aftermarket parts purchases for U.S. and Japan markets) as the baseline for their JFY 1994 sourcing goals announced strictly in terms of OE purchases.

JAMA statistics also do not allow analysis of purchases from traditional U.S. suppliers compared to purchases from Japanese transplant suppliers. However, data provided by the Boston Consulting Group in their 1993 report to JAMA indicates that in 1992 traditional U.S. suppliers, i.e., non-Japanese owned companies, supplied 26 percent of the components sourced by Japanese owned U.S. vehicle assemblers. The majority of U.S. parts purchases reported by JAMA for U.S. use are supplied by Japanese transplant suppliers.

JAPANESE PURCHASES OF U.S. AUTOMOTIVE PARTS

	Millions of dollars									Annual Percentage Changes							
MOSS CATEGORY	JFY 1985	JFY 1986	JFY 1987	JFY 1988	JFY 1989	JFY 1990	JFY 1991	JFY 1992	1st Half JFY 93	JFY 1985-86	JFY 1986-87	JFY 1987-88	JFY 1988-89	JFY 1989-90	JFY 1990-91	JFY 1991-92	1st Half JFY 92-93
Engine parts	205.8	238.5	317.5	375.9	707.1	1,050.8	1,372.2	1,638.0	763.7	15.9%	33.1%	18.4%	88.1%	48.6%	30.6%	19.4%	4.1%
Chassis parts	187.9	205.5	286.5	532.2	892.8	1,193.6	1,480.7	2,141.8	1,195.4	9.4%	39.4%	85.8%	67.8%	33.7%	24.1%	44.6%	33.8%
Body parts	396.4	776.0	1,057.3	1,821.5	2,732.5	3,353.4	4,021.2	5,194.6	2,761.5	95.8%	36.2%	72.3%	50.0%	22.7%	19.9%	29.2%	20.3%
Electrical parts	684.5	916.2	999.0	1,326.5	1,779.4	2,246.4	2,416.9	3,140.3	1,586.3	33.8%	9.0%	32.8%	34.1%	26.2%	7.6%	29.9%	15.3%
Accessories	76.0	106.5	88.5	217.7	202.6	210.9	232.0	284.2	212.7	40.1%	-16.9%	146.0%	-6.9%	4.1%	10.0%	22.5%	92.5%
Materials	175.9	246.7	386.6	634.7	807.3	1,019.2	1,004.9	1,219.7	717.1	40.3%	56.7%	64.2%	27.2%	26.2%	-1.4%	21.4%	26.1%
Total	1,726.5	2,489.4	3,135.4	4,908.5	7,121.7	9,074.3	10,527.9	13,618.6	7,236.7	44.2%	26.0%	56.6%	45.1%	27.4%	16.0%	29.4%	21.1%

Notes: Parts are for use in both Japan and the United States. The Japanese fiscal year is April 1 to March 30.

Source: Japan Automobile Manufacturers Association

U.S.-JAPAN AUTO PARTS TRADE DATA

The United States auto parts industry is competitive internationally as evidenced by its $28.5 billion in total parts exports in 1992, an increase of over 60 percent since 1988. In 1988, U.S. parts exports were valued at $17.5 billion and imported parts stood at nearly $31 billion, for a global imbalance of $13.5 billion, some $8.8 billion of which was attributed to the U.S. parts trade deficit with Japan ($401 million of U.S. exports vs. $9.3 billion Japanese imports).

By 1992, except for a $9.8 billion parts trade deficit with Japan ($1.0 billion U.S. exports vs. $10.8 billion Japanese imports), the U.S. would have enjoyed a $4.7 billion global parts trade surplus. Cumulative data for the first three quarters of 1993 indicate a worsening of the bilateral parts trade imbalance. The third quarter U.S.-Japan parts trade deficit of $8.25 billion, when annualized for calendar year 1993, could reach $11.0 billion.

Although U.S. parts exports have grown 17 percent, or $3.7 billion, over the same period in 1992, and are outpacing the 14 percent import growth rate, the $8.25 billion deficit with Japan will deny the U.S. what otherwise would be a three quarter 1993 global parts trade surplus of $5.0 billion.

U.S. AUTOMOTIVE PARTS TRADE, 1988-1992

(in millions of dollars)

Selected Countries	EXPORTS 1988	EXPORTS 1989	EXPORTS 1990	EXPORTS 1991	EXPORTS 1992	IMPORTS 1988	IMPORTS 1989	IMPORTS 1990	IMPORTS 1991	IMPORTS 1992	BALANCE 1988	BALANCE 1989	BALANCE 1990	BALANCE 1991	BALANCE 1992
TOTAL	17,418	17,457	22,856	24,130	28,484	30,966	32,009	31,699	29,846	33,534	(13,548)	(14,552)	(8,843)	(5,716)	(5,051)
Australia	275	359	318	284	357	54	60	53	52	74	221	298	265	232	283
Belgium	187	196	235	236	266	74	103	78	78	58	113	93	157	158	209
Brazil	134	142	129	106	150	1,175	794	702	661	562	(1,041)	(652)	(573)	(555)	(411)
Canada	10,460	9,830	13,676	13,575	15,282	9,268	9,383	9,093	7,972	8,995	1,192	448	4,583	5,602	6,286
China, PRC	16	24	26	55	83	36	57	94	159	259	(20)	(33)	(68)	(104)	(176)
Colombia	80	77	86	90	131	0	3	3	4	5	80	74	83	86	126
Denmark	6	8	17	37	20	8	9	12	12	12	(2)	(1)	6	25	7
EC	1,464	1,458	1,701	1,839	2,206	4,453	4,226	4,391	3,860	3,927	(2,989)	(2,768)	(2,690)	(2,020)	(1,721)
France	229	133	164	159	224	812	751	823	823	797	(583)	(618)	(659)	(664)	(572)
Germany	393	411	459	571	714	2,153	1,879	2,088	1,805	1,908	(1,760)	(1,468)	(1,628)	(1,234)	(1,194)
Greece	8	10	12	8	11	2	0	0	1	0	6	9	12	8	11
Hong Kong	N/A	24	50	60	79	84	162	168	83	96	N/A	(138)	(118)	(23)	(17)
Ireland	9	8	8	12	11	12	31	5	5	6	(3)	(23)	3	7	4
Italy	71	79	128	144	134	386	409	426	352	359	(315)	(331)	(297)	(208)	(224)
Japan	451	619	871	826	1,035	9,293	10,595	10,418	9,963	10,821	(8,842)	(9,976)	(9,547)	(9,137)	(9,786)
Korea, Republic of	170	159	204	356	356	609	683	685	577	647	(439)	(524)	(481)	(221)	(291)
Luxembourg	3	11	7	9	6	1	5	8	2	5	2	6	(0)	7	1
Mexico	2,749	3,312	4,302	5,103	6,515	4,617	4,461	4,464	4,890	6,203	(1,868)	(1,150)	(162)	213	312
Netherlands	104	122	147	159	204	40	47	43	51	31	64	75	105	108	172
Portugal	6	5	4	6	6	11	15	13	13	13	(5)	(10)	(8)	(8)	(7)
Saudi Arabia	185	176	162	269	248	0	0	0	0	0	185	175	162	269	248
Singapore	N/A	83	104	99	119	118	120	124	206	229	N/A	(37)	(19)	(107)	(110)
Spain	29	28	43	66	82	300	334	306	232	210	(271)	(306)	(263)	(166)	(128)
Sweden	89	103	131	119	121	108	118	120	118	130	(19)	(15)	11	1	(9)
Taiwan, ROC	79	115	113	122	158	650	625	606	529	627	(571)	(510)	(493)	(407)	(469)
United Kingdom	419	448	475	432	527	654	640	590	485	527	(235)	(192)	(115)	(53)	(0)
Venezuela	411	139	165	299	398	0	32	57	53	66	411	108	108	246	331
All others	855	838	818	927	1,244	501	724	779	772	959	354	114	39	155	285

Customs value, exports f.a.s. and general imports data

Source: Automotive Parts & Suppliers Division, Office of Automotive Affairs, International Trade Administration, U.S. Department of Commerce
Compiled from U.S. Census Bureau data

U.S. AUTOMOTIVE PARTS TRADE

January-September 1989-93

(in millions of dollars)

	EXPORTS					92-93	IMPORTS					92-93	BALANCE				
Selected Countries	QIII 89	QIII 90	QIII 91	QIII 92	QIII 93	% Chg	QIII 89	QIII 90	QIII 91	QIII 92	QIII 93	% Chg	QIII 89	QIII 90	QIII 91	QIII 92	QIII 93
TOTAL	12,974	17,105	17,761	21,134	24,810	17	24,074	24,111	21,782	24,680	28,068	14	(11,100)	(7,006)	(4,020)	(3,546)	(3,257)
Australia	272	249	201	266	350	31	47	40	36	51	57	11	225	210	165	215	293
Belgium	143	171	183	193	253	31	78	58	56	43	58	35	66	113	128	150	195
Brazil	99	98	63	106	157	48	621	522	515	419	540	29	(522)	(424)	(452)	(313)	(383)
Canada	7,243	10,276	10,128	11,398	13,854	22	7,033	7,102	5,816	6,602	7,580	15	210	3,175	4,312	4,796	6,274
China, PRC	19	18	31	53	137	160	36	66	106	188	236	26	(17)	(49)	(75)	(135)	(100)
Colombia	56	68	68	82	136	65	2	2	3	4	4	(8)	54	66	65	78	132
Denmark	7	14	31	17	10	(40)	6	8	8	9	8	(17)	0	6	23	7	2
EC	1,101	1,249	1,385	1,647	1,811	10	3,241	3,304	2,897	2,855	3,030	6	(2,140)	(2,055)	(1,512)	(1,209)	(1,219)
France	96	121	114	164	169	3	561	604	632	596	610	2	(465)	(483)	(518)	(431)	(441)
Germany	307	334	412	536	588	10	1,433	1,586	1,326	1,369	1,473	8	(1,126)	(1,252)	(914)	(833)	(884)
Greece	7	10	7	7	6	(9)	0	0	1	0	0	57	7	9	6	7	6
Hong Kong	17	35	38	57	88	55	113	135	67	66	80	21	(96)	(100)	(29)	(9)	8
Ireland	6	6	11	7	10	39	22	4	4	5	2	(50)	(16)	2	7	3	8
Italy	60	84	124	110	69	(37)	305	325	275	255	286	12	(244)	(241)	(150)	(144)	(217)
Japan	427	624	612	755	831	10	7,941	7,740	7,287	7,972	9,081	14	(7,515)	(7,116)	(6,674)	(7,217)	(8,250)
Korea, Republic of	123	151	270	260	308	18	502	522	427	469	490	4	(379)	(371)	(157)	(209)	(182)
Luxembourg	9	6	7	5	4	(15)	4	6	2	3	10	208	5	(0)	5	1	(6)
Mexico	2,504	3,198	3,650	4,910	5,243	7	3,353	3,456	3,464	4,622	5,307	15	(849)	(260)	186	288	(64)
Netherlands	92	114	118	148	196	32	36	32	28	24	26	9	56	83	89	125	170
Portugal	4	3	4	5	3	(43)	12	9	9	10	7	(27)	(8)	(6)	(6)	(5)	(4)
Saudi Arabia	135	122	188	191	198	3	0	0	0	0	0	60	135	122	188	191	197
Singapore	58	77	73	86	106	23	91	89	140	172	173	0	(33)	(12)	(67)	(86)	(67)
Spain	23	27	47	61	67	10	264	233	186	154	168	9	(241)	(206)	(139)	(93)	(101)
Sweden	76	102	92	83	88	7	87	92	86	96	106	11	(11)	10	6	(13)	(18)
Taiwan, ROC	89	91	85	110	162	47	473	463	390	470	525	12	(384)	(372)	(305)	(360)	(364)
United Kingdom	349	360	327	394	435	10	501	438	371	388	381	(2)	(152)	(78)	(44)	7	54
Venezuela	110	125	217	297	276	(7)	23	42	40	50	52	5	88	83	178	248	224
All others	646	622	659	832	1,067	28	511	535	508	643	807	26	134	87	151	189	259

General imports, customs value, and exports f.a.s. data

Source: Automotive Parts and Suppliers Division, Office of Automotive Affairs, ITA, U.S. Department of Commerce
Compiled from U.S. Census Bureau data

NEW STUDIES

1993 USTR TRADE BARRIERS REPORT

The Office of the United States Trade Representative's 1993 National Trade Estimate on Foreign Trade Barriers contributed significantly to the new Clinton Administration's high level focus on U.S.-Japan auto parts trade. It concluded:

> **"Close and durable intercorporate relations make it difficult for foreign auto parts suppliers to compete with traditional Japanese suppliers for business from Japanese automotive manufacturers.**
>
> **Since 1986, the U.S. and Japanese governments have been working together under the MOSS framework to improve market access for foreign suppliers. In 1990, the two Governments agreed on a Market-Oriented Cooperation Plan (MOCP) intended to facilitate the development of long-term business relations between Japanese automotive manufacturers and U.S. auto parts suppliers. In 1991, an MOCP work plan was developed to define and expand specific MOCP activities. In response to U.S. pressure, Japanese auto manufacturers have issued and periodically updated import expansion and U.S. supplier outreach programs. Japanese vehicle makers announced in January, 1992, an intensified effort to expand U.S. auto parts purchases by 1994 beyond goals set only two months earlier.**
>
> **In addition, the Japanese Government announced plans for assistance to U.S. auto parts firms seeking business with Japanese automotive companies, improved import expansion incentives, and resolved long-term differences with the United States on certain automotive certification and homologation standards. Since January, 1992, two surveys of Japanese parts sourcing activities with U.S. components makers have been undertaken. Those surveys indicate that, although Japanese firms have shown greater interest in discussing business deals, few sales have resulted.**
>
> **A Department of Commerce sponsored study of the Japanese auto parts aftermarket showed that safety regulations pertaining to the licensing of vehicle repair facilities and mechanics in Japan, among other factors, limited access to the Japanese aftermarket for U.S. auto parts manufacturers.**
>
> **In 1992, Japan's auto parts market was estimated at more than $95 billion, while its domestic auto sales were 4,454,012 units. The U.S. share of the auto parts market remains less than two percent, and by some measures, less than one percent. Only 37,085 U.S. autos were sold in Japan in 1992, almost half of which were produced in Honda's Ohio plant."**

FUSS, MURPHY AND WAVERMAN STUDY

The research group of Fuss, Murphy and Waverman at the University of Toronto examined factors affecting productivity in the Japanese and U.S. automotive markets for a report on The Competitiveness of the North American Automotive Industry, prepared for the U.S.-Canada Automotive Select Panel by the Office for the Study of Automotive Transportation in June 1992.

According to the Report:

> "Their results suggest that the U.S. Industry may have achieved a slight cost advantage over Japan in 1988, moving from 55% higher costs in 1984 to almost five percent lower costs in 1988, primarily because of the substantial revaluation of the yen dollar exchange rate."

The research noted that: "Most of this U.S. advantage is due to 19% lower input costs from supplier industries . . . ."

U.S.-CANADA AUTOMOTIVE SELECT PANEL

The U.S.-Canada Automotive Select Panel issued its report, Competitiveness of the North American Automotive Industry in June 1992. According to the Report, the Panel's focus is to assess the nature and magnitude of the recent decline in the North American automotive industry's competitiveness, identify key reasons for the decline and the related implications, and recommend both private and public sector initiatives to reverse the trend.

To assure full trade reciprocity the panel urged the following immediate attention to trade with Japan:

> "The issues raised by trading patterns between North America and Japan that have developed over the last two decades require immediate government attention. Past negotiations on these issues have proven unsuccessful. A new approach is required to address what has become a serious problem after two decades of procrastination and delay. In January 1992, an excellent step in this direction was initiated by President Bush when he traveled to Japan and made economic and trade issues the focal point of this trip. Government action is needed to build on this initiative.
>
> It is imperative that specific government action be taken to address the current trade imbalance between North America and Japan. The process by which the trade relationship between the U.S. and Japan is defined must be refocused to ensure that steps are taken that allow the relationship to become one that is free and fair. Government-to-government negotiations between the U.S. and Japan must reach closure on a plan to reduce rapidly the

existing $43 billion trade deficit (of which over 70 percent is automotive related). The plan should focus on specific steps that will be taken by Japan to increase substantially each year its imports of manufactured goods as a percent of apparent consumption and otherwise to achieve meaningful and measurable progress toward annual reductions in the deficit.

Government-to-government negotiations between the U.S. and Japan with respect to the automotive sector also should be initiated. These should be aimed at specific actions the Japanese can take over the next 12 to 18 months to reduce the automotive trade imbalances. These might include:

Eliminating the remaining formal and informal barriers to North American vehicle access to the Japanese market, and encouraging purchases of such vehicles at levels that will dissipate the cultural bias in Japan to buy Japanese.

Rapidly increasing the level of business with proven North American-based suppliers by changing the level of expectations of existing Japanese keiretsu suppliers in North America and Japan in regard to growth and business share.

Within the working levels of the Japanese vehicle manufacturers, increasing the desire to purchase components and engineering services from traditional North American-based suppliers.

Expanding the aftermarket channels for auto parts on Japanese vehicles beyond the existing Japanese-controlled dealership network in both North America and Japan.

Government negotiations addressing the above issues should establish mechanisms for monitoring and measuring annual progress against each recommended action item, including commitments made during the President's trip to Japan. Involvement of North American industry representatives in addressing, resolving and implementing solutions to the above issues should represent a critical element of the government's initiatives.

In the event that steps to meet the above actions are not taken or progress toward meeting them is insufficient, U.S. government action should be taken to enforce vigorously existing trade laws. To the extent that existing legislation is insufficient to address the elimination of unfair trade practices, new legislation should be crafted to provide for sufficient remedies."

ECONOMIC STRATEGY INSTITUTE STUDY

The Washington D.C. based Economic Strategy Institute (ESI) released its report, The Future of the Auto Industry, in January 1992.

The report provided detailed findings supporting its conclusion that U.S. auto makers can compete: "After 40 years of losing market share, the U.S. automotive industry has become a world-class competitor on a current operating basis." The study cites U.S. auto makers' world leadership in areas including fuel economy, innovation, technology, safety, price, and cost (current operating).

ESI argues that "concern for the fate of the industry is justified because of its size and the impossibility of replacing its contribution to U.S. living standards. It accounts for:

- **4.5 percent of GNP and nearly two million jobs.**
- **Double the U.S. average value-added per employees.**
- **Over 25% of all sales of rubber, lead, iron stampings, machine tools, glass and semiconductors.**
- **12.4 percent of all corporate research and development and 6.4 percent of employed scientists and engineers.**
- **Surveys show that one-third of workers displaced from this and other related industries remain unemployed after three years."**

Concerning U.S. suppliers, ESI found that "the U.S. auto parts and components industry is by a wide margin the low-cost producer." ESI estimates that the current U.S. parts and materials advantage per small car assembled is $3,389 versus $4,124 in Japanese-brand parts needed."

ESI adds that transplants continue to source most parts from Japan, "despite the decisive cost advantage of U.S. parts and component makers." ESI projects that "Of the $10 billion in new Japanese purchases of U.S. parts announced during the President's trip to Japan, actual U.S. content will be only $2.6 billion."

AMERICAN CHAMBER OF COMMERCE IN JAPAN

The American Chamber of Commerce in Japan's (ACCJ) 1993 United States-Japan Trade White Paper cites major obstacles to U.S. firms, including two of particular concern to U.S. parts makers, exclusionary business relationships and Japanese failure to enforce anti-monopoly rules. According to ACCJ President Richard J. Johannessen, Jr., "The White Paper suggests that, despite Japanese Government actions to liberalize and internationalize,

76-349 O - 95 - 4

years of protection and export-driven strategies have shaped an environment inherently unfavorable to foreign firms."

Concerning U.S.-Japan automobile trade, the ACCJ requested Japanese Government action to address issues, involving accessibility to the Japanese automotive distribution system for U.S. manufacturers, modified homologation requirements, and commodity tax and other tax issues.

The White Paper's automotive component section states that "A great deal of effort has been exerted by both Japanese automobile manufacturers and U.S. component manufacturers towards significantly redressing the trade imbalance. Activity within the last year has brought about many new purchase inquiries and opportunities to start the process of gaining new business."

The report cites a number of inter-industry initiatives promoting the design-in process. However, it cautions that "only a few cases exist today in which U.S. suppliers are included in the supplier associations that play such a vital role in component design. The ACCJ also contends that the issue of pricing should be addressed. "There are clear examples of pricing differences between products sold in the U.S. and in Japan by the same Japanese company, which indicate predatory practices." The report concludes: "A higher price in Japan is quite common and would support the suggestion that transplant auto parts companies are being subsidized to the detriment of U.S. traditional suppliers." ACCJ also calls for enhanced Japanese patent protection without which U.S. suppliers' technological leadership may be lost to Japanese suppliers.

The ACCJ recommends that MITI be "encouraged to play a stronger role with JAMA. Targets for increases of purchases should be closely monitored, especially those from traditional U.S. auto parts suppliers." Strong involvement by both governments is urged to "continue working to resolve these issues to ensure that the targets set in January 1992 are met."

THE CHANGING STRUCTURE OF THE U.S. AUTOMOTIVE PARTS INDUSTRY

In a broad review of changes in the U.S. automotive parts industry during the past 15 years, Sean McAlinden and Brett Smith of the Office for the Study of Automotive Transportation include information and analysis of the impact of the huge U.S. automotive trade deficit and the location of production facilities in the U.S. by Japanese assemblers and parts producers. The paper specifically states, though, that it does not address trade patterns or trade issues directly.

One finding of the study was that the number of supplier establishments increased by 1300 between 1979 and 1991, but employment fell by 196,000, or 24 percent. The increase in the share of assembled vehicles imported into the U.S. was the major factor in the

employment decline, as productivity increased only slowly. Transplant suppliers accounted for nearly one fifth of the new plants. Their choice of the Midsouth for significant share of investment has helped shift the industry's employment more toward that region. The market share held by domestic output has increased in recent years along with output by the transplant assemblers, but this has not translated into increased parts industry employment. Transplant parts producers account for about 8 percent of industry employment. The number of Japanese parts firms locating in the U.S. has fallen dramatically in recent years, so it is hard to predict the contribution of transplant auto parts producers in the future.

WHITE PAPER ON THE JAPANESE AUTOMOTIVE AFTERMARKET

The Japan Automotive Advisory Group, a group of some 75 senior Japanese based executives of majority U.S.-owned automotive suppliers, released its 1993 study of trade conditions in Japan's automotive aftermarket. Regarding OEM dominance of Japan's aftermarket, JAAG observed:

> **"A pricing structure as rigid as that seen in the Japan automotive aftermarket would normally suggest opportunities for financially strong and high-volume parts suppliers to bypass existing wholesaler and jobber levels of the distribution channel and sell directly to repair shops and users. However, the formidable strength of the Japanese OEMs (Original Equipment Manufacturers) with their structural control of a large part of the distribution chain, represents a very strong barrier to this type of marketing strategy.**
>
> **It is significant to note that the OEM channel, with the possible exception of gas stations, reaches into virtually every channel of the total market through their OES (Original Equipment Supplier) Regional Parts Centers and appears to control over 80 percent of the automotive aftermarket. This share can vary from line to line, with some lines controlling about 50 or 60 percent, while others may control as much as 100 percent of the aftermarket. But 80 percent is felt to be a valid estimate of the overall OEM share of the automotive aftermarket in Japan when all lines are considered.**
>
> **In order for parts suppliers to penetrate and sell through the OEM distribution system, the company must first be accepted by each OEM as a potential supplier for a given vehicle model and then must go through an expensive and lengthy approval process. Without a strong, independent automotive aftermarket channel, it is extremely difficult for outside suppliers to economically penetrate the Japanese automotive aftermarket."**

JAAG identified a number of key opportunities for change. With respect to Japan's "Shaken," or vehicle inspection system, the study notes that the "repair and inspect" system is based on the concept that a vehicle must not fail inspection, and thereby encourages replacing any suspect part with genuine-OE parts before inspection. Of some 19,000 garages designated to handle inspections, 8,000 are owned and/or controlled by OE manufacturers which use only OE-genuine parts. "No one else is authorized to do this work, again, demonstrating the dominance of the OEM in the automotive aftermarket," according to JAAG.

JAAG recommends a shift to an "inspect and repair" regime as opposed to "repair and inspect" and the study concludes:

"Only parts that actually fail inspection would then be replaced. Such a change should lead to fewer parts needing replacement and would open the market for comparable non-OE parts that could adequately pass inspection standards. As stated before, under the current system, dealers and consumers are not inclined to use non-OE parts for fear of failing the 'Shaken' inspection.

Access to qualified inspection could be widened by allowing 'Shitei Kojo' (designated garages) to approve work done by 60,000 'Nintei Kojo' (authorized repair garages), which are more inclined to choose independent aftermarket parts suppliers to improve profit margins.

It is suggested that MOT encourage recognition of 'Doitsu Sei' (comparable) non-OE parts as substitutes for genuine-OE parts during 'Shaken' Inspection."

JAAG also recommends:

"Suggest MOT change regulations to allow any service facilities employing certified mechanics (Yushikakusha) to supervise and verify DIY repairs/replacement of underbody and other parts and to widen the role of authorized repair shops by relaxing conditions for installation of these parts. Further, it is suggested that the current requirement for MOT inspection within 15 days be eliminated for DIY repairs that have been verified by a certified mechanic."

Other opportunities cited include:

"The 'Doitsu Sei' or 'Similarity Principle' standard is currently defined rather vaguely. It is suggested that MOT encourage recognition of 'Doitsu Sei' (comparable) non-OE parts. This should be based on being functionally equivalent without sacrificing safety.

Additionally, it is suggested that the principle of 'self-certification' be established and, in a more formal way, develop a system or a 'mark of acceptance' as a symbol to represent 'Doitsu Sei' parts. JAPA's 'Yuryou' mark is one example; there may be others.

All foreign companies wishing to enter the market should be advised by MOT of all procedures relating to Government acceptance of their product(s) for approval in the 'Shaken' system."

BIBLIOGRAPHY OF MAJOR REPORTS

Auto Parts Advisory Committee to the United States Department of Commerce and the Congress, Overview of U.S. Automotive Parts Trade With Japan: An Interim Report to the Secretary of Commerce, Washington, D.C., December 1990.

Auto Parts Advisory Committee to the United States Department of Commerce and the Congress U.S. Automotive Parts Trade With Japan: 1991 Annual Report to the Secretary of Commerce, Washington, D.C., February 1992.

Auto Parts Advisory Committee to the United States Department of Commerce and the Congress, APAC Review of Alternative Trade Policies Background Paper, Washington, D.C., February 1992.

American Chamber of Commerce in Japan, 1993 United States-Japan Trade White Paper, Tokyo, Japan, 1993.

Economic Strategy Institute, The Future of the Auto Industry: It Can Compete, Can It Survive?, Washington, D.C., 1992.

General Accounting Office, United States Congress, Foreign Investment, Growing Japanese Presence in the U.S. Auto Industry, Washington D.C., March 1988.

Japan Automotive Advisory Group, White Paper on the Japanese Automotive Aftermarket, Tokyo, Japan, 1993.

Office for the Study of Automotive Transportation, University of Michigan Transportation Research Institute , The U.S.-Japan Bilateral 1993 Automotive Trade Deficit, Ann Arbor, Michigan, September 1989.

Office for the Study of Automotive Transportation, University of Michigan Transportation Research Institute, The U.S.-Japan Automotive Bilateral 1994 Trade Deficit, Ann Arbor, Michigan, May 1991.

Office for the Study of Automotive Transportation, University of Michigan Transportation Research Institute, The 1996 U.S.-Japan Bilateral Automotive Trade Deficit, Ann Arbor, Michigan, July 1993.

Office for the Study of Automotive Transportation, University of Michigan Transportation Research Institute, The Changing Structure of the U.S. Automotive Parts Industry, Ann Arbor, Michigan, 1992.

United States Automotive Parts Industry Japan Office, Japan Automotive Insight, Tokyo, Japan, Published Monthly.

United States-Canada Automotive Select Panel, Competitiveness of the North American Automotive Industry, June 1992.

United States-Canada Automotive Select Panel and Office for the Study of Automotive Transportation, University of Michigan Transportation Research Institute, The Competitiveness of the North American Automotive Industry, Ann Arbor, Michigan, June 1992.

United States Department of Commerce, Fact Sheet: Market-Oriented Cooperation Plan for Transportation Machinery (Automotive Parts), Washington, D.C., June 15, 1990.

United States Department of Commerce, U.S. Industrial Outlook, Washington, D.C., Published Annually.

United States Department of Commerce, Foreign Direct Investment in the United States, Washington, D.C. Published Annually.

United States Department of Commerce, Japanese Direct Investment in U.S. Manufacturing, Washington, D.C., August 1991.

United States Department of Commerce and Japanese Ministry of International Trade and Industry, Structural Impediments Initiative, the Joint DOC/MITI Price Survey, Washington, D.C., December 1989

United States Department of Commerce and A.T. Kearney, Distribution System of the Japanese Auto Parts Aftermarket, Washington, D.C., June 1991.

United States Department of Commerce, Summary Analysis, DOC/MITI Automotive Parts Price Survey, Washington D.C., June 27, 1991.

United States Government and Government of Japan, Final Report on the MOSS Talks on Transportation Machinery, Washington, D.C. August 18, 1987.

United States Government and Government of Japan, SII Working Group, Joint Report on the Structural Impediments Initiative, Washington, D.C. June 28, 1990.

United States Government and Government of Japan, Annual Report on the Structural Impediments Initiative, Washington, D.C. May 1991.

United States International Trade Commission, U.S. Global Competitiveness: The U.S. Automotive Parts Industry, Washington, D.C., December 1987.

United States International Trade Commission, Phase I: Japan's Distribution System and Options for Improving U.S. Access, Washington, D.C., June 1990.

United States Trade Representative, Annual Report to the President of the United States on the Trade Agreements Program, Washington, D.C., Published Annually

A Developing Framework for US-Japan Automotive Trade: Challenges, Competitive Survival, and Significance

Written Testimony before the
United States Senate
Committee on Governmental Affairs
Subcommittee on Oversight of Government management
Washington, D.C.
February 3, 1994

Michael S. Flynn
Research Scientist, Associate Director
Office for the Study of Automotive Transportation
University of Michigan Transportation Research Institute

This testimony addresses a number of specific issues relating to the current trade negotiations between the United States and Japan in the automotive sector, the so-called "Framework Negotiations." My remarks draw on some recent analyses my colleagues and I have performed on the competitive situation of the North American automotive industry. I will limit my remarks to three issue areas. First, the importance and likely future developments in bilateral automotive trade, particularly in the light of recent competitive developments. Second, what levels of economic activity in the automotive supplier sector does vehicle assembly generate and how might it differ between Big Three and Japanese-affiliated assembly operations in the United States? Third, how might we objectively measure the U.S. supplier content of vehicles so that we can determine a baseline for assessing change?

I should say at the outset that I find the basic premise of the automotive Framework negotiations promising. As I understand it, the first step is to develop reasonable measures of the current situation, so that both Japan and the United States are addressing the issue from a common understanding, if not perspective. Such a jointly recognized measure would, I believe, permit more fruitful and beneficial negotiations as to progress in deficit reduction, methods of deficit reduction, and a common frame of reference for resolving outstanding issues. I am somewhat disheartened to note that much of the public debate has degenerated to disputes about targets, goals, and pledges, and about which country now adheres more closely to free trade principles.

I must also say that I increasingly find the comparison of the Japanese and U.S. automotive manufacturers less and less useful. We have reached the point where the achievements and strategies of the companies are so different within each industry, and the comparisons of companies across industries so variable, that it is difficult to lump them together into national industries for some purposes. I think this is especially true of the Japanese companies in North America, where the sourcing patterns—especially increased sourcing from traditional U.S. suppliers—are quite different across the companies. I believe that some of the Japanese companies are quite sincere in their efforts to increase sourcing from traditional U.S. suppliers, whether to avoid friction or to seek economic advantage. On the other hand, some still seem resistant, lacking in serious effort to consider fairly the performance and advantages these suppliers offer.

The bilateral U.S.-Japan automotive trade deficit

Let me summarize the key points and findings from a study we completed last summer:

1. The automotive trade deficit continues to have major implications for overall U.S. trade performance: at just over $50 billion, it accounted for about 60 percent of the total U.S. merchandise deficit in 1992, some 11 percent more than it accounted for in 1990, although it fell some $9 billion compared to 1990.

2. The composition of the total automotive deficit has altered significantly, with the parts' share growing from 7 percent in 1985 to 19 percent in 1992, in spite of a substantial decline from 1989, when part share was 27 percent.

3. In spite of the yen nearly doubling in strengthen from 1985 to 1992, the current dollar automotive trade deficit with Japan increased 30 percent over that period and now accounts for about 62 percent of the total automotive deficit. The deficit of $31.5 billion in 1992 has been essentially stable for three years.

4. The growth in the bilateral deficit since 1985 has been almost entirely due to trade in parts. The parts share of the bilateral deficit increased from 19 percent to 35 percent, and, at $10.9 billion, offsets an 1992 automotive parts surplus of some $1.2 billion with the rest of the world. The bilateral parts deficit now reflects Japanese parts imports to the United States of $11.86 billion, and U.S. parts exports to Japan of $930 million. Those 1992 U.S. parts exports of $930 million represent almost a quadrupling since 1985.

5. Our scenario method for projecting the 1996 bilateral vehicle deficit results in four forecasts, all assuming that Japanese vehicle sales are sourced 55 percent in North America and 45 percent from Japan. Our 16 million market, stable Japanese share case calls for unit imports from Japan to rise 7 percent, while the increase in U.S. vehicle exports to 100,000 units (an increase of some 145 percent) results in a deficit that rises just over 19 percent, to about $24.38 billion constant 1992 dollars. Our 15 million market and Japanese share falling 3.4 points case sees Japanese unit imports down some 12 percent, U.S. exports tripling to 120,000 units, and the constant dollar deficit falling to $19.2 billion, down just over 6 percent. The value and units of Japanese vehicle imports do not move in lockstep because the Japanese industry is exporting more expensive vehicles to the United States as they enter more lucrative segments of the market.

6. Increased transplant production will drive the parts trade deficit, but we still expect that deficit to fall by 1996, after increasing in 1993 through 1995. In our strong market, stable Japanese share scenario, parts imports for 1996 will reach $12 billion 1992 dollars. This is up 1 percent from 1992 levels, although the market and total Japanese sales in the United States are each 24 percent larger. In our average market, shrinking Japanese share scenario, parts imports in 1996 will reach just over $11 billion 1992 dollars, down 6.5 percent from 1992, although the market is 16 percent larger, and Japanese sales rise 1 percent.

7. Our combined forecast for vehicle and parts bilateral deficits for 1996 yield a constant dollar deficit ranging from $34.95 billion, up 11 percent from 1992, to $27.97 billion, down about 11 percent. The parts share of the total deficit accounts for 30 to 31 percent of the total.

The news for the traditional domestic industry has indeed been good of late. The Big Three regained about 2 points of production share in 1993, are enjoying improved profit performance, appear to have substantially reduced the quality advantages of Japanese nameplates, and now enjoy a price advantage over comparable Japanese vehicles. The market continues to shift to light trucks, a segment where Big Three share is over 86 percent, and away from cars, where their share is a more modest 60 percent. For the nation, there is the added good news of a continued increase in the share of Japanese nameplate sales that are sourced here in the United States or in Canada, rather than Japan.

However, the return of better times to Detroit in and of itself will not eliminate the national problem of that troublesome deficit. Our trade projections assume a growing light truck share, and we developed scenarios that set Japanese share loss at over three points. In spite of these favorable developments for the Big Three, our scenarios forecast a continuing, although perhaps slightly easing bilateral trade deficit through 1996. Nor will increased sourcing of Japanese sales from U.S. operations substantially reduce that deficit in the next few years.

Moreover, the continuing economic difficulties of Japan and some very real challenges faced by the Japanese industry make it unlikely that the changed economics of automotive production, now tilted in favor of the United States, will result in a smooth transition to a more open Japanese market in parts and vehicles. In particular, the Japanese manufacturers' understandable preference for supporting their traditional suppliers in Japan and affiliated operations in the United States will continue to pose immense access problems for fully competitive traditional U.S. suppliers. We also expect to see a reduction in the number of new models and an extension of the product life cycle in Japan, thus slowing any natural increase new models might spur in the sourcing of parts and components to traditional U.S. suppliers.

Suppliers of Parts and Components

A knotty aspect of the bilateral automotive deficit is the role of the Japanese-affiliated operations of the Japanese manufacturers and their traditional suppliers, drawn here in large numbers in the late 1980s to serve their customers. Some see these activities as an important part of the eventual solution—reduction of the trade imbalance, as they essentially replace imported automotive goods from Japan. Others see them as an enduring part of the problem because of their high Japanese import content and low U.S.—especially traditional U.S.—supplier content. Whatever their eventual role may be, there is little question that they contribute to the problem today, and will continue to do so for some years to come.

These operations, by all reports, rely upon substantially lower U.S. part and component content, and substantially higher Japanese import content than do the Big Three and traditional U.S. suppliers. However, it is difficult to estimate exactly what these levels may be, especially since anecdotal evidence suggests that they are changing rapidly, at least for some of the Japanese manufacturers' affiliated U.S. operations.

This "domestic content" is important because it determines the "multiplier" effect for the basic operations of vehicle assembly. There is no question in my mind that the U.S. economic activity generated by the Big Three at traditional suppliers exceeds that generated by Japanese-affiliated U.S. manufacturers to a substantial degree. Moreover, the sourcing patterns determine the kind of supplier work performed, and I believe it is critical that the United States maintain a technically sophisticated automotive supplier industry. We are too large an economy, and auto suppliers play too important a role in our economy, to be simply another industry's source of less expensive labor.

In 1991 we performed a case analysis of Honda's sourcing, basing this work on publicly available and OSAT collected information. I must stress that we selected Honda, not to hold them up for particular criticism, but because we felt that Honda probably had the highest level of domestic sourcing, and their lead in U.S. production might suggest how other Japanese-affiliated manufacturers would source production parts and components as they increased volumes and gained U.S. experience. Our analysis confirmed Honda's high levels of domestic content, but at 62 percent, rather than the near 75 percent often reported in the press at that time. We estimated that some 16 percent of the total value of the vehicle was sourced from traditional U.S. suppliers, while Japanese-affiliated suppliers accounted for 26 percent and Honda's own U.S. operations for another 20 percent. The balance, or 38 percent, was imported. If we examine only the sourceable content—purchased parts and components—20 percent come from traditional U.S. parts suppliers, 33 percent from transplant suppliers, and 48 percent from offshore sources.

Our statistical analysis associated $3,345 of imported Japanese auto parts with each vehicle assembled at Japanese-affiliated operations in the United States during 1992. This represents an increase of more than $300 in parts imports compared with our 1990 result—a 5 percent increase, compounded annually. If we assume a 3 percent inflation rate over the last two years and corresponding indexed wages, then there was virtually no change in transplant import content from 1990 to 1992. Moreover, the average value of Japanese-affiliated production increased over the same period, as intermediate passenger cars rose from 43 percent to 64 percent of the production mix. These data, then, suggest that there probably has been some replacement of imported parts by domestic U.S. parts production. However, the level of import content is still extremely high, especially since Big Three production was not reliably related to Japanese parts imports in 1992.

We will soon publish a series of forecasts through the year 2003, based on expert opinion of members of the U.S. industry, including both traditional and Japanese-affiliated manufacturers and suppliers. While our respondents are certainly not always correct in their forecasts, their forecasts do reveal their planning assumptions. These participants estimate the U.S. sourcing of Japanese-affiliated manufacturers at about 20% currently, and rising just to 21% by 2003, as most of the increased North American sourcing goes to Mexico. By contrast, they estimate that the Big Three currently source 60% in the United States, falling to 44% by 2003, but still more than twice the level of the Japanese-affiliated assemblers.

We also performed an analysis of the change in composition of U.S.-Japan automotive parts trade. These results suggested that fast-growing Japanese exports through 1991 could be characterized as high-value, while fast growing U.S. exports could be characterized as low value. Similarly, our case study results suggested that U.S. suppliers to Honda were underrepresented in high value subsystems like the engine and transmission, and overrepresented in lower value systems, like hardware and interior trim.

The engineering work required for automotive production is sophisticated and well-paying, and therefore engineering activity should be considered an important economic benefit of an automotive industry. Our forthcoming forecasts series estimates that the Big Three currently perform 90% of their engineering for North American production in North America, probably falling to 80% by 2003. Japanese-affiliated manufacturers are estimated to perform about 10% here currently, rising to 25% by 2003.

Finally, the traditional U.S. supplier still finds it extremely difficult to penetrate the Japanese original equipment parts market, the largest single-nation parts market in the world since 1981. While parts exports from the United States to Japan have grown rapidly, they still totaled less than $1 billion in 1992. Our surplus with the rest of the automotive world makes it as difficult to believe that this reflects a free economic market as it is to believe that less than 1% vehicle share in Japan simply reflects consumer preference.

Measurement of U.S. content

Analysts and companies report a variety of numbers that intuitively appear related to the bilateral automotive trade deficit. Thus, a manufacturer may label the "U.S. content" of a particular vehicle, based on its material and part (but not assembly) content; or report that it is a "domestic" vehicle (75 percent U.S. and Canadian content) under Corporate Average Fuel Economy (CAFE) standards, which covers most costs. The manufacturers may also claim tariff-free crossing of the U.S.-Canadian-Mexican borders under NAFTA, with its specific content tracing requirements, or report the total volume of "auto parts and materials" purchased for export to Japan. While all of these trade numbers do relate to the bilateral automotive trade deficit, they do so in different, and often complicated, ways. Even trade data has its pitfalls, as the U.S. government relies on two different sources, and the U.S. and Japanese governments use different methods for valuing imports.

It is not surprising that U.S. government numbers typically suggest lower exports of U.S. automotive parts and components to Japan than do the numbers often cited by Japanese companies and trade associations to demonstrate their commitment to higher levels of sourcing in the United States. JAMA and MITI release figures on the purchase of U.S.-made parts by Japanese automotive firms on a regular basis that are sometimes referred to as part of the "MOSS Data Collection." Figure 1 displays the published reports of these purchases on a Japanese fiscal year basis for 1986-1991 and the first half of 1992, as well as U.S. government totals for the full calendar years 1986-1992.

Figure 1 shows the JAMA/MITI totals of Japanese manufacturer's total purchases of U.S.-made parts rising from a level of $2.5 billion in FY1986 to a level of $10.5 billion in FY1991, with an encouraging $6.7 billion for the first half of FY1992. We estimate, based on these figures, that automotive part and component exports to Japan from the United States rose from $400 million in FY1986 to a total of $2.1 billion in 1991, or a five-fold gain. However, the U.S. ITC reports that exports of automotive parts to Japan rose four-fold, but from a lower base of $203 million in 1986 to $835 million in 1991. These two 1991 estimates are just about $1.25 billion apart, and undoubtedly bear on the different evaluations the two countries—and industry members—make about the rate and level of progress in opening the Japanese parts market to U.S. sales.

We think most of the difference in these estimated exports to Japan is due to different definitions of automotive parts and components. The definitions used by the ITC to report automotive parts trade target discrete products, generally used in the final assembly of major automotive components or the vehicle itself. On the other hand, the JAMA/MITI—and Japanese manufacturer—definition of automotive parts appears to incorporate purchases of other goods and products by automotive companies. These include both raw materials (such as aluminum ingots), paint, plastic resins, and other products (such as textiles for carpeting and leather for seat covers) that have many non-automotive uses. To be sure, these non automotive purchases and exports are recorded by the ITC, but in other product categories. Thus, such purchases count as U.S. exports in determining the overall bilateral trade balance, but they are not counted in the calculation of the specific automotive trade balance.

76-349 O - 95 - 5

These differences in definition reflect differing concerns and information. From the view of a Japanese company, it makes perfect sense to record as an automotive purchase and export those materials and products that they buy for use in automotive production in Japan. From the view of the U.S. government, it is more efficient and accurate to simply record the product and categorize it by general use, rather than to make its categorization dependent on determining its final specific use.

Figure 1
Japanese Purchases of U.S. Automotive Parts
1985-1992

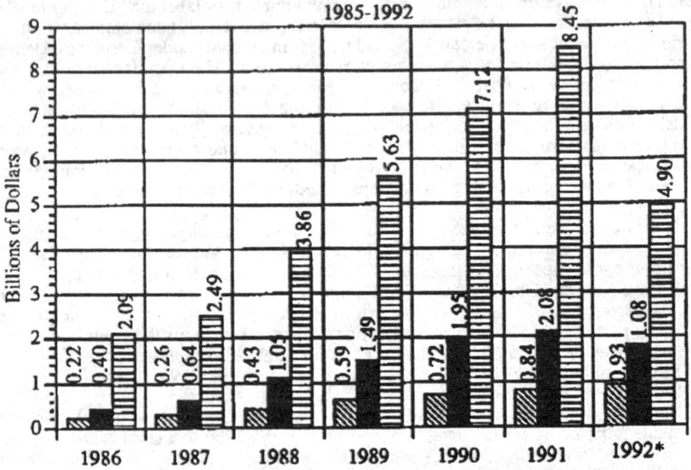

* 1992 data: ITC figures are for entire year, JAMA figures are for 1st half.

ITC Exports to Japan (Calander Year) | JAMA Exports to Japan (Fiscal Year) | JAMA Local Use (Fiscal Year)

Source: Japanese Automobile Manufacturing Association, U.S. International Trade Commision

However, these numbers do suggest a problematic pattern in the development of U.S. automotive-related exports. First, the ITC's more restrictive definition of automotive parts suggests that automotive exports to Japan have increased, reaching a level of over $800 million by 1991. Second, since we assume that the JAMA/MITI numbers typically include the trade flows reported by the ITC, we can recover an estimate of trade developments for automotive-related, but non automotive goods. Subtracting the ITC numbers from the JAMA/MITI numbers suggests that the exports of automotive-related goods have grown from some $200 million to $1.25 billion, or over 600 percent, from FY1986 to FY1991. Thus exports of ITC-defined automotive goods fell from 51 percent of the JAMA/MITI FY1986 total to 40 percent of the FY1991 total.

These non automotive goods are typically both lower value and lower value-added than automotive goods as defined by the ITC. Moreover, they are often produced by companies less reliant on their automotive business than those that produce automotive goods as defined by the ITC. Therefore, the economic and industry implications of increased exports to Japan are quite different for the ITC and JAMA/MITI estimates.

While we think that most of the disagreement between ITC and JAMA/MITI export estimates is rooted in these differing definitions, we do think it is possible that JAMA/MITI numbers occasionally *double-count* purchases. For example, the purchase of steel in the United States that is used to fabricate a part or stamping in a U.S. facility may be properly counted as a domestic-use purchase. However, the full value of the exported part or stamping—including the value of the steel—may also be counted as an export. Such double-counts are difficult to avoid, and thus would not be especially surprising if they in fact occur.

JAMA and MITI also report Japanese manufacturers' total purchases of U.S. automotive parts for use at their facilities in the United States. These purchases reached $8.45 billion in FY1991, up four-fold compared with FY1986 purchases. This estimate raises an immediate question: why has such an increase in purchases, culminating in such a high level, seemingly not affected the parts trade deficit? While these purchases are not exports, one might expect that to some extent they substitute for imported parts.

There are many reasons why these JAMA/MITI domestic-use numbers might be so at odds with U.S. government reports of the bilateral deficit. First, the production of Japanese vehicles in the United States more than doubled from 1986 to 1991, increasing the total U.S. purchases. Second, these probably include purchases that would be treated as "automotive" in an input/output analysis of the economy, while U.S. trade data include only discrete automotive parts. If we apply the same percentage figure that we calculated for exports in 1991, we would expect about $3.4 billion of this total to represent automotive parts and components as defined for trade purposes and general economic analysis.

Third, at least some of the Japanese companies include purchases from U.S. companies that originate outside the United States in their estimates of U.S. purchases. Thus, if the Japanese manufacturer sources parts from a GM plant for use in Japan, those are counted as U.S. exports to Japan—even if they come from GM facilities in Canada, Mexico, Europe, or Asia. This may be an important source of the differences in export numbers reported by JAMA and the U.S. ITC.

Fourth, in line with CAFE content calculations, U.S. assembly plants typically count as "U.S." content the full value of parts and components shipped from U.S.-sited plants, without determining the actual U.S. content of such shipments. Thus an air conditioner shipped from a component facility in the United States would be treated as 100 percent U.S. content by the automaker, even if most of its value is composed of an imported Japanese component, such as a compressor. Import content, as measured for CAFE purposes, is often lower than import content measured in trade terms.

Fifth, there may be some double-counting of purchases for strictly domestic use. If aluminum is purchased for the production of engine blocks or heads at a Japanese affiliated engine foundry, its value as a raw material is properly included. But that value may be counted again if the engine is sold to the assembly plant and also counted, at full value, as a domestic use purchase. Again, such double-counting would not be surprising.

Our estimate above assumed that the ratio of automotive parts to total purchases is the same for export and domestic consumption. However, we suspect that the sourcing of more restrictively defined automotive goods may in fact be somewhat higher for U.S. assemblies than for export to Japan. Such sourcing differences would make sense for bulky, heavy, and low-value parts: they would not be candidates for export from either country to the other. Can we estimate the proportion of these purchases that are automotive in the more restrictive sense?

We estimate the current dollar capacity of Japanese-owned, U.S.-sited supplier facilities at about $4 billion, based on estimated employment of 56,000 in 1991, and automotive supplier industry average output per worker of over $70,000. Of course, these facilities also sell to the Big Three, and many are experiencing severe problems of under-capacity. If we assume that as much as 80 percent of this capacity supplied Japanese-owned, U.S.-sited facilities, then these facilities might account for about $3.2 billion in U.S. purchases of automotive parts and components. Perhaps a more realistic estimate of 60 percent of capacity would suggest $2.4 billion in purchases.

We estimated that traditional domestic suppliers accounted for just under $1,600 in value per unit at Honda. While we recognize that the Japanese manufacturers have undoubtedly increased their sourcing of automotive parts from traditional U.S. suppliers, we doubt that this source had reached $1,600 on average by 1991, since Honda produces a more expensive vehicle. U.S. produced Honda cars are generally thought to have higher levels of U.S. content than the average of all new entrant assembly plants. However, if the average level of traditional U.S. supplier content is as high as $1,300 per unit, then 1991's Japanese-controlled production in the United States of 1.55 million vehicles would have yielded just over $2 billion in U.S. content. If traditional supplier content was still as low as $1,000 per unit, that would yield $1.5 billion in 1991 U.S. content.

The combined low and high estimates for Japanese-affiliated and traditional suppliers suggest that $4 to $5 billion in U.S. purchases of restrictively defined automotive parts and components is reasonable, while $8.45 billion is highly unlikely.

We prefer the broader definitions and categories of automotive trade used by JAMA, especially if combined with a tracing requirement as is the case for NAFTA duty-free movement. They more closely approximate the approach of input-output analysis for measuring the relationship, linkages, and importance of an industry to the total economy than do the discrete part definitions used by the U.S. government. Common, consistent, and accurate measurement would make these data useful for cost-benefit analyses, and would facilitate agreement between the two governments on the nature, extent, and perhaps even seriousness of the trade problems they face.

I would like to close this testimony be repeating a policy recommendation that we included in our most recent trade analysis, one that supports the purpose and spirit of the Framework negotiations: *The U.S. and Japanese governments should establish a shared and standardized definition of automotive and automotive-related goods and services, and ensure that automotive trade flows are measured accurately, reliably, and consistently.*

It seems to me that this would be a useful and effective first step in bringing about eventual resolution of bilateral trade friction. Until the two governments use the same baseline, it is difficult to see how they can move forward in negotiations.

AAMA
American Automobile Manufacturers Association

1401 H Street, N.W., Suite 900 • Washington, D.C. 20005
Tel. No. 202-326-5500 • Fax No. 202-326-5567

Andrew H. Card, Jr.
President and Chief Executive Officer

Testimony of

ANDREW H. CARD, Jr.

President and Chief Executive Officer

AMERICAN AUTOMOBILE MANUFACTURERS ASSOCIATION

before the

Senate Committee on Government Operations

February 3, 1994

AMERICAN AUTOMOBILE MANUFACTURERS ASSOCIATION

Testimony before the

Senate Committee on Government Operations

February 3, 1994

My name is Andrew H. Card, Jr., President and CEO of the American Automobile Manufacturers Association. AAMA is the trade association of America's Car Companies, Chrysler Corporation, Ford Motor Company, and General Motors Corporation. Our companies employ more than 730,000 American men and women, accounting for 19 of 20 U.S. jobs engaged in building automobiles. Together with our dealers and suppliers, our industry employs 2.3 million Americans.

Prior to joining AAMA, I had the honor to serve as Secretary of Transportation during the Bush Administration and earlier served both Presidents Bush and Reagan in a number of positions within the White House staff.

Chairman Levin and members of the Committee, I want to thank you for the opportunity to testify here today. I also want to express appreciation for your continued leadership in bringing automotive trade with Japan to the forefront of the public agenda. Having just returned from Tokyo this weekend, I can assure you that the public's interest in the status of the Framework negotiations is far greater in Japan than it is here.

As you know, within the current bilateral Framework negotiations, which are addressing the overall U.S.-Japan trade deficit, there is a separate and distinct negotiation concerning the extraordinary trade imbalance between the U.S. and Japan in automobiles and auto parts. While American car manufacturers are deeply involved and supportive of the negotiations relating to auto parts, I will focus today on trade in autos and trucks, because over $20 billion of the $30 billion bilateral automotive trade deficit is caused by the outlandish one-way trade in automobiles.

Mr. Chairman, I am here on behalf of America's car companies to deliver a simple four-point message:

1) America's auto makers are back and ready to meet any competition in the world;

2) Our products continue to face systematic exclusionary barriers that bar access to the Japanese market;

3) The resulting automotive trade imbalance with Japan, which accounts for one quarter of the entire U.S. trade deficit with the world, is unacceptable and must be immediately and aggressively addressed by our two governments; and

4) All previous talks with Japan over the past decade have failed to produce results. The Administration must continue to insist on a Framework agreement that provides clear benchmarks for measuring increased access to the Japanese automobile and auto parts market.

As a committed free trader, I personally reject the notion that the Administration's call for measuring results in improved market access is "managed trade"; in fact, the most glaring example of successfully managed trade in the world today is the Japanese automotive market itself, where imports from all countries -- Europe, Asia, and North America -- total only three percent of the market.

What the United States seeks in these negotiations is that the Japanese government demonstrate the same commitment and enthusiasm to creating and sustaining the conditions of a free and open market in Japan, which they so vigorously pursue in the U.S., Europe, and other major markets. Japan's government is a strong believer in free trade in every market but its own and we must stand firm in our efforts to bring the fruits of free trade to the Japanese consumer.

I. America's Car Companies Are World-class Competitive.

This is an exciting time for America's car companies. Two recessions, currency fluctuations which raised the prices of our exports, and stiff competition in our home market challenged our companies. It was not long ago that public officials were wondering how best to "save" the American auto industry, as if saving a memento of some bygone era.

Then, the most amazing thing happened: The American auto industry staged perhaps the most dramatic turnaround of any major manufacturing industry in our history. I am proud to say that the industry did it the old-fashioned way: We met our competition head on, listened to our customers, and regained the cutting edge in innovation and quality.

American consumers have responded to our products' quality, value, and innovative styling just as we hoped they would: In 1993, American auto makers' sales in the U.S. increased 10 percent over 1992, and we won significant market share back from our import competitors. "Made in America" again has become a badge of honor. Even foreign car makers who assemble cars here now proudly advertise their "American" heritage.

As Time magazine recently proclaimed in a cover story, America's car companies "are on a roll." However, our success in the world's largest car market -- the U.S. -- and in the other major markets around the globe is not duplicated in the world's second-largest car market, Japan. While Japanese car makers have had virtually unrestricted access to the U.S.

market, Japan's market is all but closed to our products. I went to Japan last week to deliver a simple message: that Japanese consumers deserve the chance and will benefit if given the same opportunity as consumers in other nations to choose from the widest variety of products -- including American cars and trucks. And, make no mistake, that opportunity does not exist in Japan today.

II. The Japanese auto market is closed to foreign car makers.

One problem that has stalled past automotive trade talks between the U.S. and Japan has been the lack of consensus on basic issues. It has been difficult for our two governments to agree on solutions when they could not even define the nature of the problems. The so-called MOSS Motor Vehicle Study, commissioned jointly by both governments and soon to be released, should finally put some of these extremely time-consuming debates about the nature of the problems in the Japanese market behind us.

The study concludes what our companies, as well as the Europeans, have been saying all along: that many factors prevent Japanese consumers from having ready and open access to imported vehicles. Those factors include an exclusive, locked dealer distribution system, policed by major financial ties between Japanese manufacturers and dealers. Moreover, the MOSS study describes a Japanese buying public that is showing significant and growing interest in purchasing foreign cars.

Because the study was commissioned and conducted jointly by both governments, its findings carry even greater weight. I wish I could show you the MOSS Study, however the Japanese government, while not disputing the findings, has not consented to releasing it.

One subject studied in great detail by the MOSS Study is Japan's auto and truck distribution system. To compare market access for consumers for automobiles sold in the U.S. and Japan, the issue of dealership arrangements is crucial because, as in other countries, a consumer seeking to buy a car must purchase it through a dealer. Japanese government and industry officials long have maintained that Japanese dealers are "free" to sell any cars they wish. The reality is that, unlike their American counterparts, Japanese car makers have deep and complex financial ties to most dealers. Thus, while it may be true that written "exclusivity clauses" now have been eliminated, the practice of manufacturer-dealer exclusivity is still plainly evident. In addition, financial links to manufacturers provide a real barrier to Japanese dealers handling imports.

While I was in Tokyo, I took the time to visit a Toyota dealership located near the American Embassy. The manager was exceedingly polite and seemed pleased for the opportunity to show me around his business. I asked him directly, "Would you sell an import? What if your customers asked you to carry American-made cars?" His answer was a still polite, but very firm, "NO!"

That answer is precisely why an automotive Framework agreement in which the

Japanese only agree to increase the number of dealers theoretically willing to sell American and other imported cars will not ensure meaningful results in the Japanese market. It is clear that, without measurable goals and objectives, most Japanese dealers would continue to focus on selling the vehicles made by the manufacturers with whom they have financial ties. Today, only six percent of all Japanese dealers sell foreign cars. But what percentage would provide adequate access? I honestly cannot provide this answer, nor do I believe officials of either government can. As in this country, the value of a particular dealership is not easily generalized, but can be individually assessed on the basis of quantity of sales, quality of service, and the old real estate axiom "location, location, location."

America's car companies only want the opportunity to enter into franchise agreements with dealerships they consider promising, without the dealers' being concerned about retribution from the Japanese manufacturers. This is precisely the way that Japanese companies entered and achieved rapid market growth in the U.S., and U.S. laws protected that right to dealer access. In a short time, Japanese companies entered into franchise agreements with thousands of Chrysler, Ford, and General Motors dealers without retribution by our companies. Such franchise agreements, by the way, typically contain sales goals, or "targets."

The Myths of Selling Cars in Japan

When all the technical and legal discussions are over, Japanese officials repeatedly tell us that American cars just are not "right" for Japan. The arguments frequently repeated unquestioned in the Japanese press are that Americans don't offer right-hand drive (RHD) models, that our cars are too big for Japanese roads, our engines are too large, the cars cost too much, and we are not committed to marketing them. Let me dispense with these in order:

Myth #1: Right-hand Drive Vehicles. Although a major share of Japanese car buyers choose to purchase left-hand drive cars, the three U.S. companies are now preparing to offer at least nine right-hand drive models in Japan. Chrysler is already selling an RHD version of the popular Jeep Cherokee, while GM offers RHD Opels. Meanwhile, a strong if limited market continues to exist for left-hand drive versions of other models, such as the Pontiac Grand Prix.

Myth #2: Vehicle Size. While I was visiting the dealership in Tokyo, I asked a customer if he would be interested in buying an American car. He said probably not because he had heard they were "too big for Japanese roads." Then he got in his Toyota Crown and drove away. The catch is that the Crown itself is larger than the Ford Taurus. I hope he comes back for a look when Ford introduces the right-hand drive version of the Taurus later this year.

Myth #3: Engine Displacement. Meanwhile, we are told that cars with engines larger than 2,000 cc, which describes most American cars destined for the Japanese market, represent less than 20 percent of the Japanese market. But 20 percent of the Japanese market is still about 1.4 million vehicles and it is the fastest growing segment in Japan, and one in which the U.S. already dominates in all other major markets. Given our current 0.3 percent market share, U.S. companies would be very happy to gain a fair portion of that 20 percent. You may be certain that, if American car companies are targeting a certain segment of the market, it is because they are already the world leaders in that segment everywhere but Japan.

Myth #4: American Marketing Efforts. Making major financial decisions about marketing efforts in a systematically closed market has been a classic "chicken and egg" dilemma. MITI officials charge that Americans don't sell cars in Japan because we do not commit seriously to doing so; we respond that it is difficult to justify major expenditures in a market you know is closed. There are too many other promising markets around the world competing for attention. Just look at changes in the whole Eastern Bloc, Asia, and Latin America. Our companies responsibly commit the shareholders' capital when there is a fair and reasonable expectation of return on that capital, future growth, and ultimate profitability.

Nonetheless, even though Japan's market remains closed today, American car makers have committed to making the substantial marketing investments needed to increase sales in that country. All three companies are putting in place the resources -- the people, plans, and marketing strategies -- that will expand sales opportunities in Japan if the market is opened.

While all of these issues have long been the subject of debate between U.S. and Japan, I am pleased to tell the Committee that the soon-to-be-released MOSS Motor Vehicle Study will confirm much of the comments European and American manufacturers have made in the past. We urge the Japanese government to allow this study to be released promptly so that, rather than collect dust in the library with hundreds of other studies of our mutual trade problem, it can actively and productively contribute to the Framework negotiation process.

III. Japan's $60 billion trade imbalance with the U.S. must be addressed.

AAMA strongly supports President Clinton's initiative to engage the Government of Japan in a serious new effort address the strains in our economic and trade relationship. The Administration to date has clearly demonstrated in these negotiations that the U.S. government and industry are determined to reverse the grossly imbalanced pattern of our trade relations with Japan. The hard reality is that the U.S. trade deficit with Japan reached $60 billion in 1993 and remains the most serious, unresolved and chronic problem in America's relationship with all of its trading partners.

Every Administration since President Nixon has recognized the danger and tried to address this growing trade imbalance. But after twenty years of discussions, hundreds of studies of the problem, major exchange rate adjustments and endless negotiations, U.S. trade with Japan remains extraordinarily imbalanced at unacceptably high levels, destroying confidence in the open global trading system that has brought prosperity to most of the world economies over the past three decades.

During my visit to Tokyo, Japanese officials often urged me to look at the "big picture." The big picture that I see is one of a intractable economic issue between the two most developed economies in the world that threatens to divide two allies if it is not addressed. In this case, I will allow the numbers to tell the story.

In 1986, when President Reagan and Prime Minister Nakasone initiated the MOSS talks, the U.S. auto trade deficit with Japan stood at $32 billion [Exhibit 1]. Last year, when President Clinton and Prime Minister Miyazawa announced the Framework for Economic Cooperation, the auto trade deficit reached an estimated $34 billion. For 1993, the auto trade deficit accounted for over half of the bilateral trade deficit, and over one-quarter of the total U.S. trade deficit with the rest of the world.

Exhibit 2 shows the export dependency of the world's three major regions of vehicle production. The U.S. and the European Community export three and seven percent, respectively, of their motor vehicle production. Japan exports 45 percent.

Finally, Exhibit 3 shows the increasing competitiveness of American car companies since 1986 evidenced by steadily rising U.S. exports to the rest of the world. Despite this trend, the top portion of the graph shows that American exports to Japan remained stagnant despite virtually constant negotiations aimed at reducing the automotive trade deficit.

President Clinton understood that a new approach to reducing the persistent trade imbalances between the U.S. and Japan was necessary. He also recognized that, in order to achieve the goal of restoring a reciprocal and balanced trading relationship, American producers must have the same access to the Japanese market that Japanese producers have enjoyed in the U.S.

IV. <u>The U.S. must not accept any proposed Framework Agreement that does not adopt measurable and verifiable results</u>.

Last April, in his first meeting with Japan's Prime Minister, then Mr. Miyazawa, President Clinton outlined the major principles which would guide his Administration's policy toward Japan:

1. In the new post-Cold war era, it is economics, not security concerns, which now require the priority attention of the two governments.

2. The Japan's trade surplus with the United States must be significantly and quickly reduced.

3. To ensure that this goal is reached, a new "results oriented" trade policy is needed, to focus on the specific sectors and structural differences in which the bilateral trade imbalance with Japan is concentrated. This new approach was embodied in the Agreement adopted by the two governments in April 1993, entitled a "Framework for a New Economic Partnership."

As you know, in the statement that initiated the Framework process, the Government of Japan specifically committed itself to achieve "a high significant decrease in its current account surplus" and "a significant increase in global imports or goods and services." For its part, the United States agreed to actively pursue the objectives of "substantially reducing its fiscal deficit, promoting domestic savings and strengthening its international competitiveness."

American carmakers believe that if these negotiations result in serious and meaningful market-opening measures in Japan, they anticipate increasing sales in Japan from a current annual base of 15,000 to more than 100,000 within three years. The Japanese are calling this managed trade; in fact, it is simply consumer opportunity. As the American car makers sell about that many cars in Indiana each year, the question is why the Japanese are absolutely stonewalling such a modest goal. We are asking for not for guaranteed sales, but opportunity; we believe our products will sell themselves if given such opportunity.

So, there is no question that American automakers are interested and committed to selling in the Japanese market. The globally competitive economics of the auto industry and the importance of the Asia-Pacific region as a future growth market alone require these commitments. The real question is, how will Japan's respond?

That question still remains very much unanswered. And that is why AAMA, along with its member companies -- Chrysler, Ford and General Motors -- are concerned that only an agreement which establishes clear and meaningful targets by which to measure whether Japan's commitment to open its market to imported vehicles and parts is worth signing.

The Framework Agreement incorporates this objective, by calling for the establishment of "objective criteria, either qualitative or qualitative or both ... to be used for the purpose of evaluating progress in each sectoral and structural area."

We support the three fundamental goals as outlined originally by U.S. negotiators that Japan must agree to cooperate in facilitating:

1) increased sales of American vehicles in Japan;

2) increased sales of American parts in Japan; and

2) increased sales of American parts in Japan; and

3) increased sales of American parts to transplants located in the U.S.

These were the Administration's original goals. We continue to support them and, if they are not achieved, we will applaud a decision to walk away from the bargaining table.

Finally, let me emphasize that neither we, nor our government is suggesting that Japanese consumers somehow be pressured or forced to buy American products. We simply seek the opportunity to reach Japanese consumers, discuss with them their questions and needs, and show them what American consumers and American workers have together created -- a wide range of quality products aimed at meeting a variety of car buyers' needs.

While in Tokyo, I had the pleasure of addressing a group of students at Keio University who had read about our cars but had never had the opportunity to experience them. I asked them, "Who should determine what cars consumers can buy?"

One student answered, *"Okyaku-sama wa kamisama desu."*

Translation: "The customer is God." I couldn't have said it better.

U.S. – Japan Automotive Trade Deficit

In Billions of Dollars

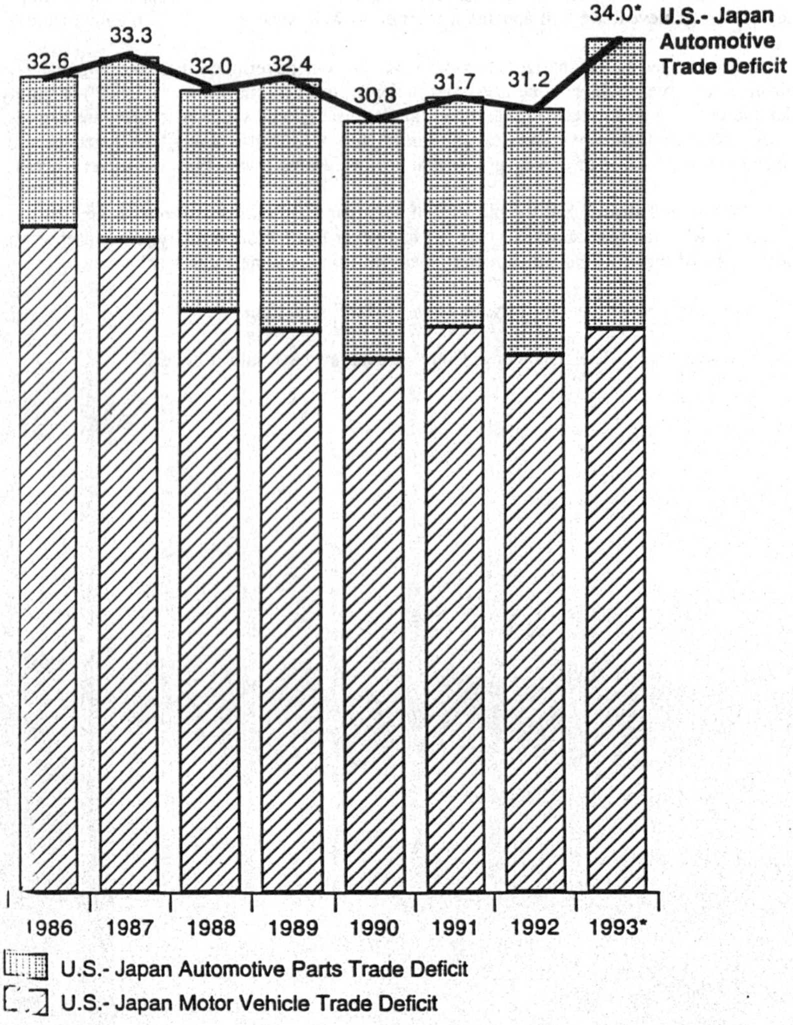

*stimated based on data through September 1993.
seasonally adjusted, current dollar basis.
urce. Office of Automotive Affairs, International Trade Administration, U.S. Department of Commerce.
mpiled from U.S. Bureau of the Census statistics.

Motor Vehicle Export Dependency – Selected Markets, 1992

(Exports as a Percent of Car and Truck Production)

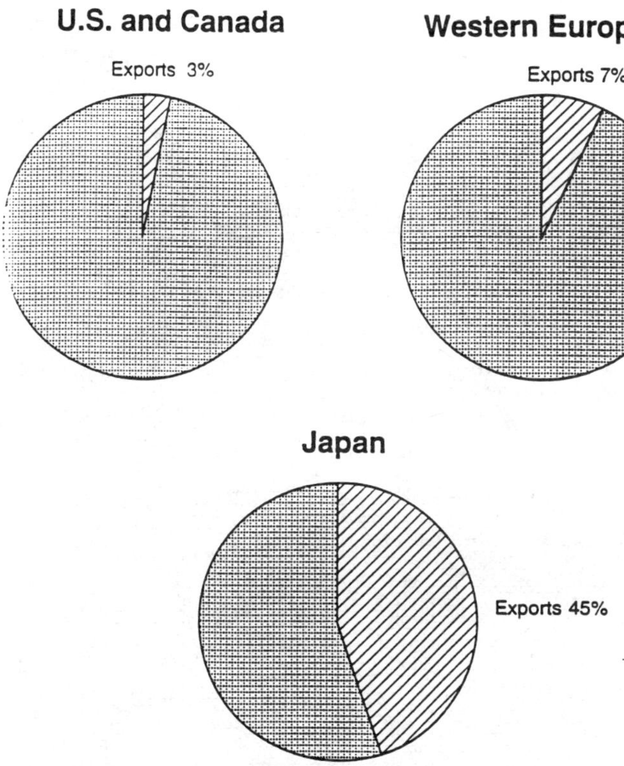

* 1991 data.
Source: American Automobile Manufacturers Association, Japan Automobile Manufacturers Association, Inc. and Hunter Publishing.

U.S. and Canadian Exports by America's Car Companies, 1986-1992*

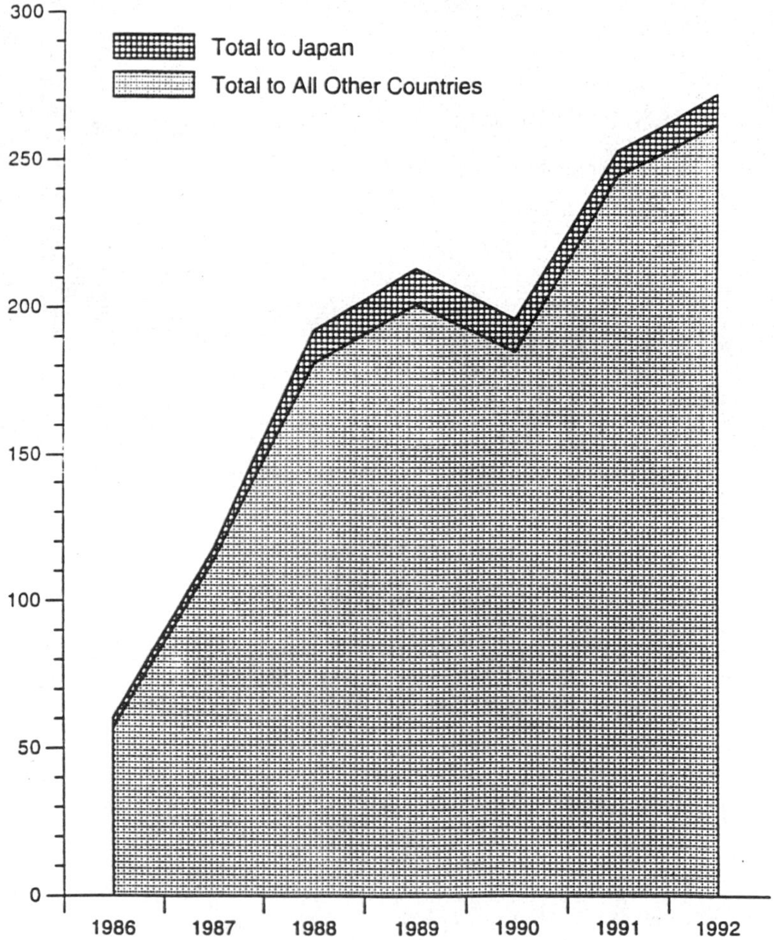

* Excludes vehicle trade between U.S. and Canada.
Source: American Automobile Manufacturers Association.

CONTENT OF A $12,000 HONDA ACCORD
BUILT AT A U.S. TRANSPLANT

	TOTAL	NORTH AMERICAN SOURCED	JAPAN SOURCED
Imported Parts	$3,820	$ 0	$3,820
Claimed U.S. Parts	$4,210		
U.S.-owned Supplier Parts		$1,585	$ 0
Parts Supplied by Japanese-affiliated parts companies in the U.S.		$2,625	
		$ 850 (32.4%)	$ 0
		$ 0	$1,775 (67.6%)
Total Parts	$8,030	$2,435	$5,595

Source: Economic Strategy Institute, The Future of the Auto Industry, 1992

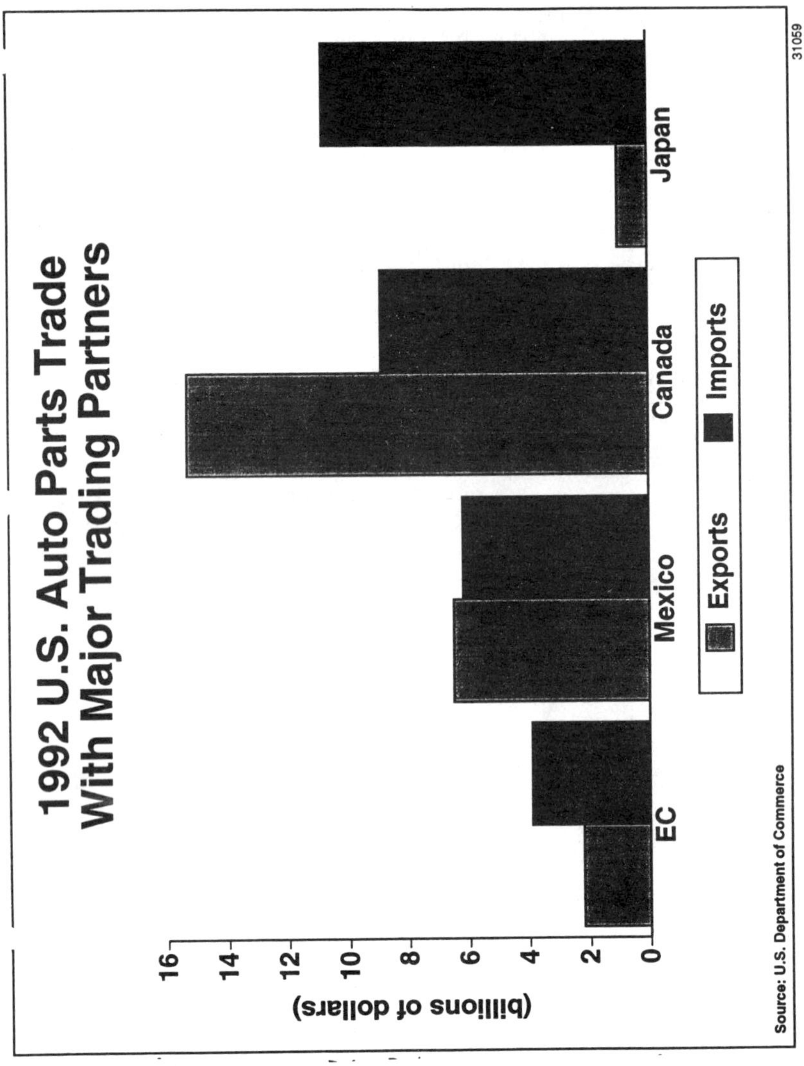
1992 U.S. Auto Parts Trade
With Major Trading Partners
(billions of dollars)
16
14
12
10
8
6
4
2
0
EC
Mexico
Canada
Japan
Exports
Imports
Source: U.S. Department of Commerce
31059

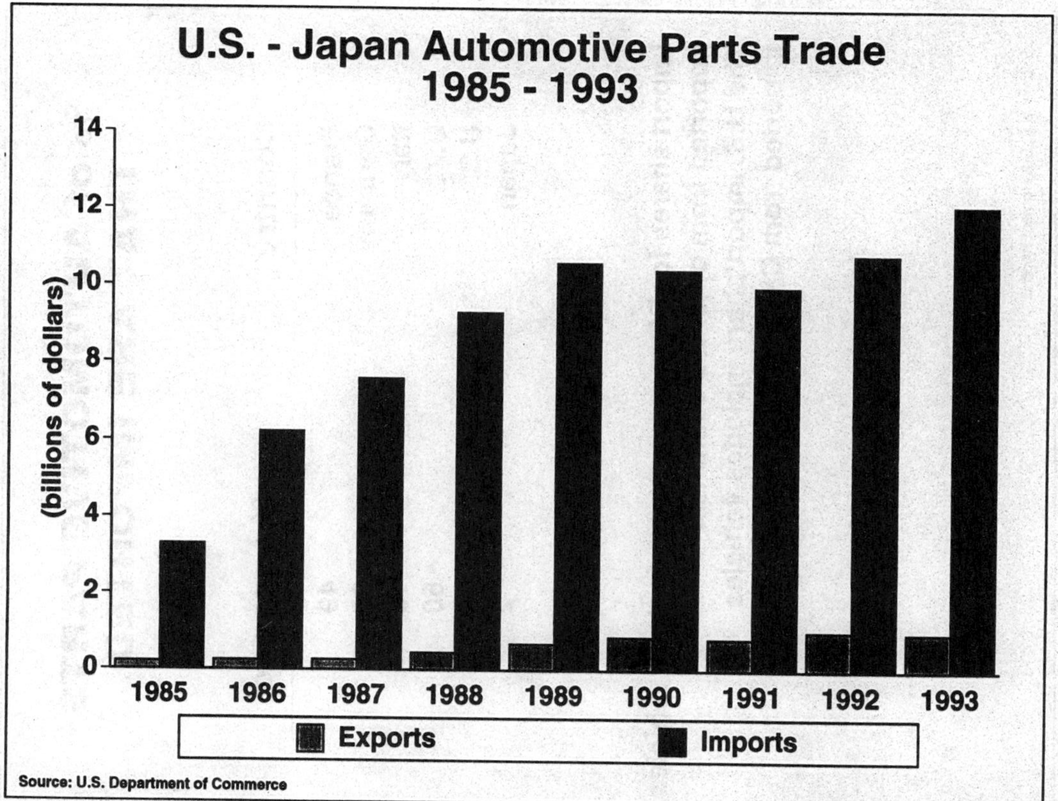
U.S. - Japan Automotive Parts Trade
1985 - 1993
(billions of dollars)
14
12
10
8
6
4
2
0
1985
1986
1987
1988
1989
1990
1991
1992
1993
Exports
Imports
Source: U.S. Department of Commerce

31059

% of AUTOMOTIVE PARTS THAT ARE IMPORTED

Country	% Imported
France	49
Germany	25
Italy	16
U.K.	60
U.S.	30
Japan	2

Import shares for EC member states include vehicles imported from other EC countries.
The U.S. import share includes vehicles imported from Canada and Mexico.

Source: U.S. Government Reports

PROMISES, PROMISES

Year	President	Promise	Approximate U.S./Japan Deficit
1971	Nixon	"Japan has accelerated its program of liberalizing its restrictions on imports."	-$1.3 bill.
1974	Ford	"The U.S. and Japan will (negotiate) to reduce tariff and other trade distortions."	-$2.8 bill.
1975	Carter	"(W)e are trying to get the Japanese to buy spare parts and parts for assembly of their own automobiles in the U.S."	-$2.9 bill.
1983	Reagan	"(W)e're encouraged by the recent commitments to further open Japan's markets."	-$21.6 bill.
1991	Bush (By VP Quayle)	"The President will take a direct message to the prime minister of Japan after the first of the year, saying that we don't anticipate continuing business as ususal."	-$43.4 bill.

Congress of the United States
House of Representatives
Washington, DC 20515

September 15, 1993

The President
The White House
Washington, DC 20500

Dear Mr. President:

As co-chairs and members of the Congressional Auto Parts Task Force, we are writing to you about the most significant component of the U.S. trade deficit with Japan: the automotive-sector deficit of $31.5 billion (in 1992), accounting for 65 percent of the total bilateral deficit.

We understand that an interagency team now is defining U.S. objectives for new auto-sector negotiations with Japan scheduled to start later this month. Based on eight years of painstaking efforts to break down Japan's auto-parts trade barriers, we believe U.S. negotiators must focus on two key objectives in order to open Japanese markets on fair commercial terms to this highly competitive segment of the U.S. auto industry.

(1) U.S. negotiators should focus on securing a commitment by the government of Japan and Japanese auto makers to increase Japanese purchases of U.S.-made auto parts by significant amounts within a definite period of time. Increased sales must be sizable enough to make a serious dent in the auto-parts trade deficit with Japan, which has risen from $3.3 billion in 1985 to nearly $11 billion in 1992 despite modest increases in sales by U.S. parts makers to the Japanese. Only once this primary objective has been secured should attention be allowed to shift to other objectives.

(2) The United States should then insist on effective measurement of progress toward meeting the agreed targets and timetables. The key point here is to track sales to the Japanese by the U.S.-based parts makers hitherto excluded from Japanese supplier networks. Purchases by Japanese manufacturers from the U.S. operations of their traditional keiretsu suppliers would not demonstrate improved market access--indeed, such purchases by themselves tend to demonstrate only the continuation of exclusionary practices by the Japanese auto industry.

We caution against putting too much emphasis on securing better data from the Japanese vehicle makers themselves. The Auto Parts Task Force has seen U.S. auto-parts initiatives diverted repeatedly over the past eight years into endless and inconclusive discussions with Japanese government and industry over the ways and means of obtaining better data from individual Japanese manufacturers. We suggest that U.S. negotiators simply tell their Japanese counterparts what measures the U.S. government will rely on in the absence of adequate disclosure by the Japanese vehicle makers. Let the Japanese government bear the burden, if it chooses, of securing the release of more reliable data from Japanese companies.

The President
September 15, 1993
page two of two

It would be of value to incorporate other measures of progress. For instance, opening Japanese automotive product-design engineering to participation by U.S.-based suppliers should be encouraged, and progress toward that goal should continue to be monitored. But the negotiations will succeed only if the two governments agree on a schedule of major, specific increases in purchases by Japanese manufacturers from traditional U.S.-based suppliers. The Japanese government should be on notice that any other outcome will trigger renewed efforts to mandate and enforce specific targets and timetables for corrective action under U.S. laws concerning unfair trade practices. After nearly a decade of talks, effective action is long overdue.

Sincerely,

MARCY KAPTUR, M.C.
Co-Chair, Auto Parts
Task Force

SANDER LEVIN, M.C.
Co-Chair, Auto Parts
Task Force

CARL LEVIN, U.S. Senator

DON RIEGLE, U.S. Senator

United States Senate

COMMITTEE ON
GOVERNMENTAL AFFAIRS
WASHINGTON, DC 20510-6250

February 3, 1994

Dr. William C. Duncan
Japan Automobile Manufacturers Association, Inc.
1050 17th Street, N.W.
Washington, D.C. 20036

Dear Dr. Duncan:

The Subcommittee on Oversight of Government Management invites you to testify at a hearing on Wednesday, February 9, 1994, which will examine the data available to determine the U.S. content of automobiles made in Japanese transplants. We would like you to testify on the data maintained by the Japanese transplant companies with respect to U.S. content. We have also invited Clyde Prestowitz, President of the Economic Strategy Institute, to testify on the same panel.

Because the lead-time for this invitation is short, I ask that you respond to Linda Gustitus, Subcommittee Staff Director (224-3682), no later than Monday, February 7th, at 9 A.M. The hearing on February 9th is scheduled to begin at 10:00 A.M. We would appreciate receiving 100 copies of your written testimony by 6 P.M., February 8th.

We look forward to having you appear. We will confirm the room number within the next few days.

Sincerely,

Carl Levin
Chairman
Subcommittee on Oversight of Government Management

CL:ljg

JAMA

JAPAN AUTOMOBILE MANUFACTURERS ASSOCIATION, INC.

WASHINGTON OFFICE

TEL. (202) 296-8537 • 1050 17TH STREET, NW, WASHINGTON, DC 20036 • FAX. (202) 872-1212

WILLIAM C. DUNCAN, Ph.D.
GENERAL DIRECTOR

<u>ORIGINAL SENT BY MESSENGER</u>

February 7, 1994

Senator Carl Levin, Chairman
Subcommittee on Oversight of Government Management
Committee on Governmental Affairs
United States Senate
Washington, DC 20510-6250

Dear Mr. Chairman:

This will acknowledge your letter of February 3, 1994, inviting me to testify at a hearing on Wednesday, February 9, 1994, "which will examine the data available to determine the U.S. content of automobiles made in Japanese transplants." You have asked that I testify "on the data maintained by the Japanese transplant companies with respect to U.S. content."

JAMA does not collect, possess or maintain data on U.S. content of automobiles made in transplant facilities in the United States. Moreover, we have no access and no authority to obtain any data the Japanese transplants may maintain with respect to U.S. content, other than publicly available information.

Therefore, we are not in a position to accept your invitation to testify about the subjects of the February 9th hearing.

Sincerely yours,

William C. Duncan

William C. Duncan, Ph.D.
General Director

United States Senate
COMMITTEE ON
GOVERNMENTAL AFFAIRS
WASHINGTON, DC 20510-6250

February 10, 1994

Dr. William C. Duncan
Japan Automobile Manufacturers Association, Inc.
1050 17th Street, N.W.
Washington, D.C. 20036

Dear Dr. Duncan:

I am in receipt of your letter dated February 7th. I was disappointed to learn that you declined my invitation to testify before the Subcommittee on Oversight of Government Management relative to the data maintained by the Japanese transplant companies with respect to U.S. content.

Your letter states that JAMA does not collect, possess or maintain data on U.S. content of automobiles made in transplant facilities in the United States. Yet the press release JAMA distributed at last week's Subcommittee hearing on auto parts trade with Japan said purchases of U.S.-made parts by Japanese manufacturers jumped from $1.7 billion in 1985 to $13.6 billion last year. The same day Honda was quoted as claiming it now uses 82 percent U.S. parts for 1994 Honda Accords build in Ohio. I find it disingenuous that JAMA and its members claim to be buying high levels of U.S. made parts but are unwilling to back-up these claims with the supporting data.

What JAMA and Honda failed to say about the figures they used is that they include a significant percent of auto parts sourced in Japan. In fact, according to a 1993 study commissioned by JAMA itself, the majority of parts purchased by transplant assemblers in the U.S. came from Japanese owned subsidiaries. A 1992 Economic Strategy Institute (ESI) study found that fully <u>two thirds</u> of the parts supplied by Japanese affiliated parts subsidiaries in the U.S. were actually made in Japan. If you claim the ESI study is wrong, please supply the data to prove it.

Your press release also called the U.S. framework proposal "shockingly discriminatory" because it requires collecting data on, and developing purchasing targets for, auto parts procurement from "non Japanese-owned companies." The focus on the national affiliation of parts companies is not because of a concern about actual ownership but because ownership is necessarily a surrogate for source of parts given the refusal of JAMA to supply the sourcing data of parts its members use. (Ironically, while you don't like references to Japanese ownership, the Japanese system of keiretsu uses Japanese ownership as criteria for being a member of the keiretsu and discriminates against U.S. owned parts companies).

The only viable alternative to tracking auto parts sales by national ownership is to track it by U.S. content levels. JAMA's refusal to provide sourcing data frustrates that alternative.

You cannot seriously claim that use of national affiliation or ownership is unfair if, when given the chance to use another, more accurate measure, you refuse to provide the data so we can make an assessment of where the parts are coming from. You can't have it both ways.

It is logical and common sensical to conclude that the reason we are not provided with the data is because the figures come out very different from what is being claimed and would show that the majority of parts in Japanese transplant vehicles in fact are made in Japan. Until we are able to verify actual U.S. made content levels in your members' transplant-built vehicles, there will continue to be serious challenges to JAMA's claims about the actual levels of claimed U.S. content and a persistent view that your refusal to provide the data is because it will undermine your own claims.

If you don't like estimates based on ownership -- supply the actual sourcing data.

Sincerely,

Carl Levin

Carl Levin
Chairman
Subcommittee on Oversight of Government Management

CL/amp

CARL LEVIN
MICHIGAN

United States Senate
WASHINGTON, DC 20510-2207

February 18, 1994

The President
The White House
Washington, DC 20500

Dear Mr. President:

I have closely followed the U.S.-Japan framework negotiations and want to congratulate you for breaking a 20 year trend of failed trade policy with Japan. This action sets an important precedent for settling for nothing less than the real and measurable opening of Japan's markets to U.S. goods.

The ball is now in our court. Since we can't open Japan's markets through a trade agreement we should now take unilateral action to pry open Japan's markets. One option under discussion is the renewal of Super 301 through executive order. Relative to that approach, may I suggest the following:

First, if you do chose to renew Super 301 through executive order, I urge you to initiate Super 301 action against Japan in auto parts trade. The private sector Auto Parts Advisory Committee (APAC) has recommended since 1991 that the administration take Section 301 action against Japan in auto parts. Doing so now under a newly restored Super 301 law would be an important first step in opening Japan's markets by investigating, exposing, and ultimately retaliating against its unfair trade practices.

Second, a Super 301 renewal by executive order should also be accompanied by a strong statement of your support for Congressional renewal of Super 301. This would allow Congress to implement a version of the "stronger sharper Super 301" you called for in "Putting People First." The Daschle/Levin Super 301 bill, S.301, represents an approach to a stronger, sharper Super 301 which I hope you will support.

Finally, in my view, the only way to pry open Japan's closed markets to U.S. autos and auto parts is to follow the European Community model of <u>imposing equivalent restrictions</u> on Japan's goods. When the European Community Japan faced the same impenetrable Japanese automotive market that we are facing, it responded by limiting the sale of Japanese vehicles in its market. We should follow the European Community model and impose limits on Japan's automotive imports into the United States. I am confident that this type of "results oriented" action will quickly result in the market opening access you seek.

I commend you for your position regarding Japan's closed markets and Japan's chronic and massive trade surplus with the United States. This deficit translates into hundreds of thousands of lost American jobs, nearly two-thirds of which are in the automotive and auto parts industry that is highly concentrated in my state of Michigan. The ultimate measure of progress will be whether the huge trade deficit between the U.S. and Japan decreases or not. By finally dealing with this trade deficit you will correct a longstanding unfair one-way street in trade.

Sincerely,

Carl Levin

Carl Levin

CL/amp
cc: Ambassador Mickey Kantor

O